PATTERNS AND SOURCES ZUNI KACHINAS

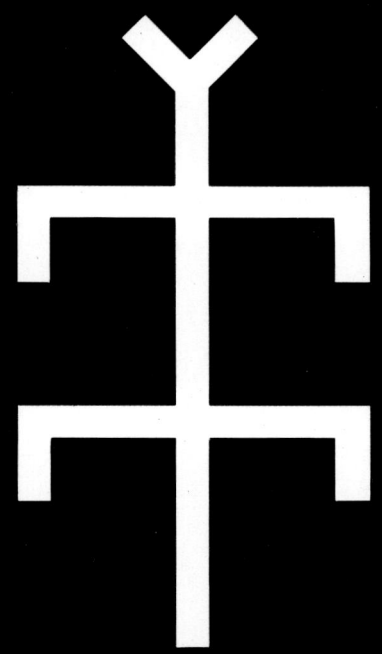

PATTERNS AND SOURCES OF ZUNI KACHINAS

Text by Barton Wright
Foreword by Bill Harmsen
Introduction by Clara Lee Tanner, LL.D.

Edited by Bill Harmsen

Published by the Harmsen Publishing Company

First published in 1988 by
The Harmsen Publishing Company
Copyright© 1988 by Harmsen Publishing Company

All rights reserved — All kachinas shown and
listed in this book are from the
Harmsen Foundation Collection

ISBN No. 0-9601322-4-4
Library of Congress Catalogue Card #87-83333

Photography by Reese Koontz, Ray Manley Studios
Printed by Arizona Lithographers
Design and typography by Raim, Incorporated
Color separations by Hollis Phototechnics

Printed in the United States of America

*Achievements in life are earned through sharing.
This book is dedicated to my partner and wife, Dorothy,
for 49 years of love, devotion and help.
I say, let's go — we have lots more to do!*
—Bill Harmsen

THE HARMSEN FOUNDATION

All of us are collectors of one thing or another, but the dedicated collector wants not only to know his subject to the nth degree — studying the background, history, origin, and the future of the artifacts — but also wants to share his amassed artifacts and knowledge with others.

Over the years, the Harmsens have collected many Indian art pieces. An exhibition of their Navajo rugs has been touring for several years with the Smithsonian Institution Traveling Exhibition (SITES). Harmsen's collections of bronzes, Indian jewelry, and paintings have also been part of museum exhibitions in the United States and Canada.

In 1983, the Harmsen Foundation was established to administer the Indian and Western art. William Jr., Robert, and Michael Harmsen also serve as members of the Board of Trustees to ensure that the collections will always be available to museums and other organizations who want to learn more about the rich culture and creative accomplishments of the American Indian.

The Harmsen Publishing Co. has also published books about the collections in an effort to share the beauty of the art with many people. These books include: *Patterns and Sources of Navajo Weaving,* with all the pieces identified as to area and time period by Dr. Joe Ben Wheat; *Sculpture to Bronze,* the story of the lost wax process with color illustrations showing the art of bronze casting, featuring the life and sculpture of Adrien Alexandre Voisin; *Harmsen's Western Americana* with a hundred biographies and color plates of some of the world's most renowned artists, art, from the Harmsen Collection; and *American Western Art,* with 125 biographies and color plates, also from the Harmsen Collection.

More than one third of the Harmsen Collection is always "on-loan" to universities, civic agencies, and public or private institutions where it becomes, in a very real sense, a public asset. The Harmsens enjoy sharing their love of western Americana with all Americans.

CONTENTS

Dedication	v
The Harmsen Foundation	vi
Foreword:	
The Whys and The Wherefores of Zuni Kachinas	viii
James C. Turpen	1
Ruth Leah Bunzel	3
Ida Poblano	4
Mary Morgan	6
Barton Wright	8
Dr. Clara Lee Tanner	9
Map of Zuni	10
Introduction:	
History and Background of Zuni Culture	12
How the Kachinas are Made	46-47
Winter Solstice	48
The Ogres	56
Initiation	60
Punitive Kachinas	68
The Quadrennial Dances	72
Shalako	80
Winter/Summer Dances	102
Dances after Shalako (Traditional Dances)	108
The Molawaia	122
Extra Dances	124
Little Dancers	137
Society Dancers	140
Conclusion	154
List of Kachinas	155

FOREWORD
THE WHYS AND THE WHEREFORES OF ZUNI KACHINAS
By Bill Harmsen

    To introduce the reason for this book and collection, I would like to make it easy and interesting for the reader to "walk through the pages" by answering some of the "whys and wherefores" that are frequently asked.

    For the past twenty-five years I have made collections of Navajo weaving, Zuni and Hopi jewelry, baskets from the Apache, Papago, Pomo, Yaqui and Hopi. I have gathered Pueblo pots, Iroquois beads, Sioux quill work, and much other art of the American Indians. This desire to collect beautiful artifacts has brought me in contact with Native American craftspeople and with many others who share the same interest, art dealers, authors, Indian traders, and students who know and love the craftwork of these people. As the collections grow, the beauty and craftsmanship of the work sharpen my desire for more knowledge about the background, history, and religious beliefs of the Indian. Why were these things created? How were the artifacts used by those who did create them? What role did they play in the social and religious lives of the people? These questions and more have led me to seek out information. In search for answers I have discovered other unusual and fascinating artifacts which have set me once more on the trail. This cycle has given my wife and me years of satisfaction as each collection teaches us more about the Native American people.

The collection shown in this book began a few years ago when Jim Turpen, a friend and advisor, showed my wife Dorothy and me a collection of 27 kachinas. These were silver-backed mosaic images of Zuni kachinas designed so they could be worn as pendants or pins, or placed upon a table or shelf as a decoration. They were made of the semi-precious stones of turquoise and jet, of coral, mother-of-pearl and other shells used by the Zuni. The collection represented the kachinas that appear in the Shalako ceremony, messengers of the gods who visit the Zuni village in early December. The pieces in the collection were inspired by the illustrations in the book *The Shalakos are Coming,* by Clara Gonzales.

Jim had spent much time in putting the Shalako kachina collection together and I was fascinated by its history and disappointed to realize that it was not for sale. Later that day, while I was looking at Indian rugs, my wife asked Jim if he would have a set of these kachinas made so that she could give the collection to me as an anniversary gift. Two years later I received twenty-seven kachinas.

In my search to find out more about Zuni kachinas, Dorothy and I again visited the Turpen Trading Company in Gallup, New Mexico. While there Jim showed me the Forty-Seventh Annual Report of the Bureau of American Ethnology, 1929-30, containing Ruth Bunzel's three-part study of the Zuni. This book included not only my twenty-seven kachinas but over a hundred others which gave me the idea of collecting all the figures illustrated by having them reproduced in mosaic and silver.

In the summer of 1984, while attending the Inter-Tribal Ceremonial in Gallup my host, Martin Link, editor of the *Indian Trader,* and Barton Wright, who was there as a judge for the Ceremonial, surveyed the expanding collection of kachinas. Having read many of Wright's books, I was interested in his thoughts about these kachinas created in a different form. The consensus of the talk was that a book of these, including the significance of each of the personages, would be the best way to share the collection with others. I could think of no one more knowledgeable or competent to help than Barton and after many meetings with him the book began to take form.

Many people pose the question, "What is a kachina?" A kachina is very difficult to define. It is a spirit being and at the same time a physical representation of that spirit in costume and mask. The masks are sacred and are handed down from generation to generation. These masks include symbolic depictions of the spirits of animals, birds, plants, elements of nature, the sun, the rain, and the clouds. The kachinas are vital for bringing rain and for the maturation of crops as well as having many other functions. They are supernaturals who visit the village in the guise of costumed dancers to bring rain and prosperity to the people. But they also encourage the children and can reprimand adults for unsuitable behavior.

Kachinas are also represented by carved wooden dolls made by the Hopi, Zuni and other Pueblo people. They are the favored subject of other arts as well and can be found in paintings, pottery, basketry, and jewelry. To the native people these other expressions are reminders of revered personages.

Kachina dolls, as they are called by non-Indians, are given to the children by the kachinas during ceremonial rites to help the children learn the meaning and importance of a particular kachina spirit. The expertly carved and painted figures at Zuni are ornamented with cloth, feathers, fur, leather, and even semi-precious stones. They are sold in trading posts, proudly displayed in museums and art galleries, and prized as possessions of collectors.

Two fine craftsmen worked on this collection. A Zuni woman, Ida Poblano, created the mosaic kachinas. Mary Morgan, a Navajo silversmith, made the silver settings. I had been under the impression that Navajo women wove rugs and blankets and Zuni women produced pottery and basketry and that the men were the silversmiths. Thus it came as a surprise to find that women in both tribes had been making jewelry for many years. It explained the fine stone work Ida was doing and the beautiful silversmithing by Mary Morgan. The second thing that surprised me was that a Zuni and Navajo were working together to create these beautiful silver and mosaic inlay kachinas.

The process of making each individual kachina requires many steps. Ida used sheet silver as a base to hold the many tiny stones that make up the mosaic. Each stone or shell used by her was individually cut and fitted onto this backing to create the colorful kachina in full ceremonial dress. When Ida had finished several she would travel to Gallup from Zuni to bring the pieces to Jim. She would then receive more directions on the next kachinas to be done. Jim would give the completed mosaics to Mary Morgan for the silver work.

Mary, a fine smith, created the silver setting for the mosaics. Using a jeweler's saw she would hand-saw the outline of a kachina from a sheet of silver. Individual pieces were then designed and cut to hold the mosaic inlay on this setting. Mary then soldered the prongs and the bezel to the setting, and hand-stamped the designs. Fastenings were soldered to the back and all pieces were polished, then the mosaic was set in place and the silver prongs adjusted to firmly hold the kachina.

As a result of the combined and dedicated efforts of these two Indian women, coupled with the guidance of Jim Turpen, this unique, first-of-a-kind collection of over 130 kachinas has been fully realized in silver and mosaic inlay. The collection is the result of the combined endeavors of the craftspeople, anthropologists, authors, and art historians who witnessed the involved ceremonies and rituals and realized their deep and rich significance.

In conclusion, I would like to say a few words about the many actors who participated in the drama of creating the collection and writing and researching the book. The star of the show is my wife, Dorothy, for encouraging me to finish the collection and this book and for her many years of inspiration and love. The supporting cast includes the following dedicated people:

Ruth Bunzel, noted Zuni authority whose historical documentation and detailed pictures included in the 47th Annual Report of the Smithsonian Institution helped inspire this collection; Jim Turpen, who inspired me with his help and enthusiasm for the Zuni way of life; Ida Poblano, whose patience and artistic talent combined with her determination created these beautiful mosaics of Zuni kachinas; Mary Morgan, whose skill as an expert silversmith and willing cooperation brought this collection to its final form; Dr. Clara Lee Tanner, an authority on Southwestern cultures, whose introduction documents the Zuni and their life style; and Barton Wright, whose research and historical knowledge have made this text informative and interesting for collector and student alike.

— Bill Harmsen

"Inspiration"

The Shalako Dancer sculptured by Jim Turpen and cast in 263 Troy ounces of sterling silver was my "inspiration." Jim Turpen's knowledge, research and enthusiasm were the motivation that led me to complete this collection and book.

JAMES C. TURPEN

Born in Winslow, Arizona in 1930, Jim Turpen came to his interest in Native Americans early in life. Jim, part Cherokee, is from a family of Indian traders; his father, uncles, and even aunts were traders with the Navajo. As a young boy he lived at the isolated trading post of Sunrise near Leupp on the Little Colorado River in the more remote western part of the Navajo Reservation. Eventually leaving there, Jim's family opened a trading business several miles east of Grand Canyon Village. Here the natural beauty of the region with its abundant wildlife and the ever present relics of ancient Indians made a lasting impression on young Turpen and stirred his latent artistic talent. Jim muses today: "The beauty of the Grand Canyon is something that cannot be forgotten, especially after having spent years with its changing moods and seasons."

Shortly after the beginning of World War II the family left Grand Canyon for Tucson where Jim finished high school and entered the University of Arizona. However, he returned each summer to work at the Grand Canyon or Grey Mountain Trading Posts on the road between Flagstaff and Cameron. During this time he met his wife-to-be, Robbie Wilson, and they were married in 1950.

Four years later Jim joined the United States Army and after training as a pilot spent his tour of duty in Germany. Upon returning to Tucson with his wife and family he continued his studies at the University of Arizona and shortly received his degree in Wildlife Management.

After graduation the Turpens moved on to Colorado where Jim was employed by IBM and Martin Marietta. However, his spare time was spent in pursuing his life-long interest in Western History, particularly as it related to Indians. He also found time to develop his talent for drawing and sculpture. Following a visit to a Taos, New Mexico foundry in 1969 he had several of his own sculptures cast in bronze. After some research he built his own foundry to cast his pieces. These works have been shown in galleries in Kansas City, Denver, Santa Fe, and Scottsdale.

In 1973 Jim and his family moved to Gallup, New Mexico to become the manager of Tobe Turpen's Indian Trading Company. Here his early experiences in trading posts and his inherent artistic ability made him an ideal person for the job. Through the years he has developed a close relationship with many of the Navajo and Zuni artisans and craftspeople. Although Jim still finds time to pursue his interests in drawing and sculpture, more and more time is spent in promoting and developing the artistic talents of the Native Americans. It was this lively interest that led to the initiation of the Harmsen Collection of Zuni mosaic inlaid kachinas.

FORTY-SEVENTH
ANNUAL REPORT OF THE

BUREAU OF AMERICAN ETHNOLOGY

TO THE SECRETARY OF THE
SMITHSONIAN INSTITUTION

1929-1930

ZUÑI KATCINAS

AN ANALYTICAL STUDY
By RUTH L. BUNZEL

RUTH LEAH BUNZEL

The inspiration for the collection of mosaic kachinas came from the publications of an anthropologist who is now ninety years old.

Ruth Bunzel was born in New York City in 1898, still maintains her residence there, and received her education in that city as well. Enrolling in Barnard College for undergraduate work, she received her B.A. in 1918 and went on to Columbia University for her Ph.D. in 1929.

Her field work and research have taken her from Mexico and Guatemala to New Mexico and Arizona and into the recesses of the Chinese community of New York City. These anthropological studies were supported by grants and fellowships from the Rockefeller Foundation, the American Social Science Research Council, and Guggenheim Foundation.

Bunzel served as a social scientist and the Director of Research in Contemporary Cultures for the U.S. Office of War Information in Washington, D.C. from 1942 through 1951. In the decade from 1960 to 1969 she was an Adjunct Professor at Columbia University and lecturer at Barnard College. Her superior work has been recognized by honors from scientific colleagues around the world, and in 1960 she was selected to edit Dr. Margaret Mead's splendid book *The Golden Age of Anthropology* (1960). She is the author of many articles and monographs and retains membership in countless professional organizations and societies.

However, it is for her work among the Zuni Indians of New Mexico that she is best known. Her field work among these people began in 1927 and covered Zuni ceremonialism, their emergence and origin myths in the Zuni language with translations into English, their ritual poetry, and an exhaustive study of their kachinas. It is this latter work, published in the *47th Annual Report of the Bureau of American Ethnology for 1929-30* (1932) and illustrated in black and white with drawings of a Zuni artist, that has served as an inspiration for the pieces in the Harmsen Collection of silver and mosaic inlay kachinas.

Dr. Bunzel is still active and a member of the Anthropology Department of Columbia University.

IDA POBLANO

Ida Vacit was born into the Pi'chikwe or Dogwood clan and for the Sus'kikwe or Coyote clan of Zuni Pueblo on December 15, 1925. While still in her teens she married a man twenty years her senior, Leo Poblano. Leo was a well-known fetish carver and produced intricate pieces of mosaic inlay that were much sought after by both museums and collectors. Through the years Ida learned his lapidary techniques and carving skills.

Tragedy struck the family on October 16, 1959 when Leo, a member of the famous Zuni fire fighting crew, was battling a blaze near Long Beach, California. Struck by a load of slurry dropped from a plane, he was suffocated. His death left Ida with four small children to raise by herself.

Through the hard years Ida made jewelry to support the family, selling her work to C. G. Wallace, John Kennedy, Dean Kirk, M. L. Woodard, Kattie Noe, and Tobe Turpen, all of whom appreciated the skills she had learned from her husband. Many of her pieces are now in fine collections throughout the country.

Although she was married to Clifford Chavez for several years and bore him three children, she continued to occupy the same little stone house she and Leo had lived in during their marriage and in which she had raised her family. Three of her daughters, Charlotte Eustace, Faye Lonjose, and Veronica Poblano have followed their parents' footsteps and are skilled lapidarists. Veronica is especially known for her renditions of Disney characters such as Mickey and Minnie Mouse, Donald Duck, and Dumbo. Ida's son Mike was also a skilled artisan.

Ida was a caring hard-working mother who liked to make quilts and do beadwork and who always seemed to have enough baked bread for the ever-growing family of children and grandchildren. In her last years, as cancer began to sap her strength and her eyesight slowly faded, her son Mike would help her cut the really tiny pieces of stone and shell. Hardly had she finished her last major project — creating the Harmsen collection of Inlaid Zuni Kachinas — when Mike died, followed a week later by Ida who passed away on January 15, 1987.

MARY MORGAN

Mary Silversmith was born into the Honaghaahnii or He-Who-Walks-Around-One clan and for the Kinyaahnii or Towering House People clan near Houck, Arizona on December 7, 1923.

Mary's early life was hard for her as she was enrolled in the Ft. Defiance Boarding School 75 miles from home for her first four school years. Because her parents were very poor and had only riding horses for transportation, they were seldom able to visit the homesick lonely little girl. However, as soon as the Houck Day School opened Mary returned home to complete the fifth, sixth, and seventh grades nearby.

Despite the fact that her mother, Regina James, was a renowned weaver young Mary did not learn to weave, feeling that it required too much hard work. When she was 13 her mother died leaving the task of raising her and her sister to her grandparents Joe and Yelthnasbah James. During this time she assisted her father, Sam Silversmith, and learned from him the intricacies of making silver jewelry.

She and Sam Begay were married in June of 1942 and four years later the family moved to Zuni where Mary worked as a silversmith for C. G. Wallace, noted Zuni trader, for seven years. In 1955 Mary and Sam and their six children returned to Houck where she went to work for Paul Stone of the Three Hogans Trading Post. Sam's increasing problems with alcoholism eventually led to their divorce in 1958.

Leaving the Three Hogans that year she went to work for John Kennedy at the Gallup Indian Trading Company. She married Frank Morgan and eventually bore seven children for him. In 1965, at the urging of Frank Thompson, Mary went to work for Tobe Turpen's Trading Company where she has remained as a master silvercraft artisan.

BARTON WRIGHT

Barton Wright, a native Arizonan, received his B.A. and M.A. degrees in Anthropology from the University of Arizona in Tucson. While working on his second degree, he excavated an Indian temple mound for the first archaeological state park in North Carolina. His experiences have been broad, including four years at the Amerind Foundation in Dragoon, Arizona immediately after graduation as an artist/archaeologist. From there he went to the Museum of Northern Arizona where, over a period of 22 years, he was curator and assistant Director of the museum. Leaving for the Museum of Man, San Diego, he served as scientific director before leaving to devote full time to his research and art interests.

While at the Museum of Northern Arizona, Barton researched and featured in an exhibition each year some facet of scientific interest from the Flagstaff area. He also staged annual Hopi and Navajo exhibits, collecting from Hopi craftspeople and Navajo Trading posts. His wife Margaret assisted in this endeavor and became an authority in her own right on Hopi silver. Wright's interest in kachinas began during the preparation of a special exhibit at the museum and was further stimulated by a knowledgeable Hopi, Jimmie Kewanwytewa. Through the years Wright has become the premier judge of kachinas in top Indian shows.

He has many publications to his credit. Foremost among these are: *Kachinas: A Hopi Artist's Documentary; Kachinas of the Zunis; Hopi Kachinas, the Complete Guide to Collecting Kachina Dolls; Hopi Material Culture;* and *Pueblo Shields.* He is continuing his research and writing in this field.

A consuming interest in art has directed Wright into additional channels. That his mother was an artist perhaps explains some of his talent. While at the University of Arizona he did much in the way of scientific illustration especially in the Department of Anthropology for Dr. Emil Haury, as well as the Geology Department. He also prepared drawings for the Forest Service, Weather Bureau, and the Royal Academy and illustrated two publications for the Amerind Foundation. During this time Wright took up scratchboard drawing for his own pleasure and has had several shows of his work as well as illustrations for a publication, *The Unchanging Hopi,* in the medium.

Barton Wright's contributions to both art and anthropology have been rich indeed. He is a charter member of the Arizona Academy of Science and has been a long-time member of the American Association of Museums, serving on their accreditation committee, and is included in *Who's Who in Western America* and *Who's Who in American Art.* But his expert knowledge behind the preparation of this Harmsen Foundation publication speaks for itself.

DR. CLARA LEE TANNER

Dr. Clara Lee Tanner, now Professor Emeritus of Anthropology at the University of Arizona, has seen a multitude of students pass through her varied courses during fifty years of teaching. Her classes have inspired her students with an abiding appreciation of Native American art. Many have continued this interest by becoming dealers, collectors, and museum specialists in the field of Indian arts and crafts. Reaching beyond the academics, her efforts have included a dozen seminal books on the craft arts of the Southwest. She has afforded direction to the public through lectures and by serving as a judge of excellence in all manner of Indian exhibitions.

A native of Biscoe, North Carolina, she was brought to the small mining town of Clifton, Arizona as a child. After studying at Arizona public schools, she enrolled at the University of Arizona as the college of her choice. She secured her B.A. degree in Archaeology and by 1928 her Masters in the same field and had been hired by the University as an Instructor in Anthropology. Through the years she gained additional breadth through graduate work at the National University of Mexico in 1929 and the Oriental Institute of the University of Chicago in 1934. Her wealth of knowledge was drawn upon in 1949 when she was visiting professor at the University of Denver and again at Colorado College, Colorado Springs, Colorado. The University of Arizona chose to recognize her many contributions in 1983 by conferring upon her a well-deserved LL.D. Although she officially retired from teaching in 1978 she has remained in demand as a lecturer and guest speaker on many Native American subjects.

The honors that she has received through the years are commensurate with her accomplishments and to mention only a few gives one some sense of their scope. In 1972-3 she was recognized as Woman of the Year by Arizona Press Women. In 1973 she received the Faculty Recognition Achievement Award from the University of Arizona Alumni Association.

Clara Lee and her husband John, whom she married in 1936, are well known to countless Native American artists and craftspeople. Through years of cooperation in events from the Gallup Inter-Tribal Ceremonial, where John is Chairman of the Judges, to the Philbrook Art Center, from numerous Indian exhibitions all over the country to state and county fairs, their contact with artists has led to mutual respect. For the Tanners it has deepened their understanding of native cultures and the aims and goals of these people. This understanding is abundantly clear in the more than ten books and 150 articles in scientific journals, popular magazines, and newspapers that Clara Lee has written. It is from this background that her introduction to the Zuni people is drawn, to provide the setting for the Harmsen Collection of mosaic kachinas.

Lying in one of the pinyon and juniper covered valleys of the coral sandstone canyons along the western flank of the Continental Divide, Zuni Pueblo was one of the earliest New Mexico towns to be bypassed. This position off the beaten path has been a boon for it has allowed the Zuni to follow their own ways relatively undisturbed.

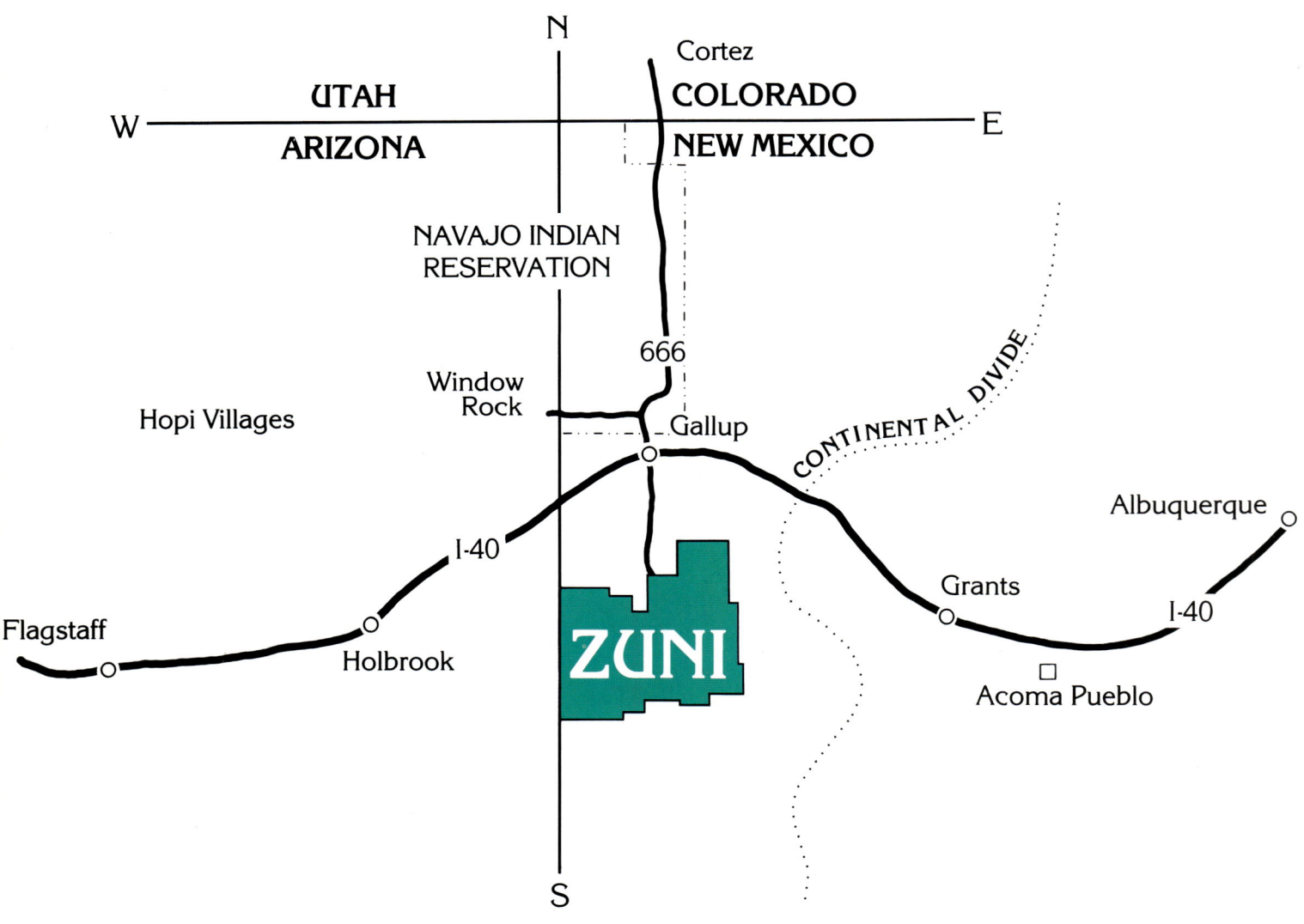

INTRODUCTION
HISTORY AND BACKGROUND OF ZUNI CULTURE
By Clara Lee Tanner

In the Beginning —

Sun Father created two sons and sent them down into the dark sunless Fourth World to lead the A'shiwi, the ancestors of the Zuni, into this world. They traveled quickly by way of Rainbows and with Lightning Arrows and Cloud Shields. Interestingly, the homes of the A'shiwi were holes in the ground and their food was grass seeds. The two young gods threw out a line of meal which "guided them to the north" and here they planted a pine tree so that the A'shiwi could climb up to the Third World. Another line of meal guided the people to the west where a spruce tree gave access to the Second World. Following a line of meal to the south, an aspen tree carried them to the First World where there was a little light reflected from the Sun's rays. A last meal line, this to the east, led to a silver spruce. Climbing this brought the A'shiwi to the "light of day place" just as the Morning Star rose above the horizon (Stevenson: 1904:24-26).

Approaching Zuni from the west is like driving into a wondrous new world. Great red sandstone cliffs serve as a spectacular backdrop for miles ahead and to right and left. Also extending for miles as one drives along this quiet roadway are rich lands for grazing, dotted here and there with juniper and pinyon. The red cliffs which get closer and closer are mindful of the distant past when the Zuni lived in comfort atop a great mesa, probably the one straight ahead.

Soon there are new houses spotted here and there, not too close to the road, with no limits to the yards. Then as one enters the village proper there are the rows of houses of depression days. Suddenly one is on the east-west main street. Off to the south are remnants of the ancient, multi-storied village, partially destroyed, partially occupied. On past are not-too-modern trading posts and stores and the village craft center, with houses beyond to right and left. Everywhere are great domed earthen ovens, the centers of activity on ceremonial occasions. On the eastern edge, as one leaves Zuni, are new government-built houses, all the same, all less than exciting after seeing a touch of the not-too-distant-past, the great pueblo. Here are small propane tanks, one for each home, each marking this section of the village as "modern." Such an introduction is ever new, no matter how many times one enters this fascinating pueblo of Zuni.

These Indians claim great antiquity for occupying this land of beauty. They relate that they came from far away, settled at many spots in this general vicinity, eventually around Hawikuh, and later established the pueblo of Zuni. Again needing more extensive agricultural and grazing areas, they spread out and established Pescado and Nutria to the northeast and east, and Ojo Caliente and Tekapo to the southwest. Settled in the nineteenth and into the twentieth centuries, these Indians returned to the mother village of Zuni on certain occasions, particularly for ceremonies. However, gradually in due time, they became permanent and self-sufficient, now returning to the mother village on very special occasions only.

Zuni Pueblo is about forty miles south of present day Gallup, New Mexico. Located here for centuries, it was known as Halona:wa at the time of the arrival of the Spaniards.

In the beginning there was a long period of non-sedentary occupation in northern New Mexico, reaching back some thousands of years. Although not in the immediate vicinity of this contemporary village, there were hunters of the great bison, mammoth, and other now extinct animals in the Plateau country, as found at Folsom, northeastern New Mexico, and at other sites along the Middle Rio Grande. Grinding stones, which are marks of seed-gathering people, have been located at sites in the Plains of San Augustin, western New Mexico. Perhaps big game hunters, with the extinction of larger animals, may have adapted to a different way of life such as seed gathering. In later years it is very likely that the seed gatherers were the first to receive corn and learned to cultivate this, and later, other produce — beans and squash — beginning perhaps as early as 1000 B.C.

Prehistoric sites of sedentary agriculturalists dot the lands for miles around later Zuni. Among others are the Village of the Great Kivas, Kiatuthlanna, and Allentown. It is likely that the ancestors of the Zuni came from one or several of these surrounding Anasazi villages. Sites in this

area clearly show a change from pit houses to surface pueblos, with all the advancements in ceramics and other crafts which occurred through the centuries in the Anasazi culture. There are also possibilities of slight Mogollon influences in this area in late prehistoric times. Eventually Zuni was occupied by descendants of some of the ancient villagers of this and nearby areas. At least the present village and several others with related people had been occupied for centuries by the time of the arrival of the Spanish under Coronado in 1540.

When the Spanish arrived, the Zuni Indians lived in the village of Halona:wa and six other pueblos. During their participation in the Pueblo Revolt of 1680 to drive out the Spaniards, they destroyed missions and killed many of these "foreigners" in their pueblos. Fearing reprisal they built new homes on top of a nearby mesa. After the Spaniards returned and re-established a Spanish Colonial government, all of these Indians set themselves up in old Halona:wa, now known as Zuni Pueblo. And so it has remained to this day. Today, the A'shiwi, the Zunis, are in their homeland, in this main village and in the surrounding settlements of Pescado, Nutria, Ojo Caliente, and Tekapo. They farm over a wide territory, and since the mid-1930s, have established many small "camps" to accommodate their livestock needs. Thus, occupation of "Zuni", permanently or for briefer spaces of time, covers a large area but all can be called "Zuniland."

Of typical pueblo style, Zuni was made up of multi-storied and adjoining rooms, some of them along open ways like short alleys, some built completely around squares or plazas (Plates 1,2,3,5). This is in evidence in these old photographs. There were a half-dozen or so such clusters or units in Zuni toward the end of the nineteenth century. The Catholic mission church was included in the largest of these plazas (Plates 2,4). House walls were built of stones, usually larger rectangular pieces chinked with smaller spalls. The stones were not too regular in shape; however, as they were plastered over, their irregularities were concealed. Some adobe was also used for structures. Construction often stressed higher buildings, two or three stories, leaving lower roof tops facing on the plazas. Here many of the inhabitants spent a good part of their time. Wooden ladders led from the ground to roof tops because often there were no ground level doors; for protection, the ladders could be pulled up in case of attack. Chimneys were often built up of no-longer-used clay pots (Plate E). Sometimes an extended upper roof gave protection to part of a roof below. Women would prepare foodstuff for storage here, drying corn, cutting lengths of squash, and preparing other produce to dry in the sun. Probably they carried on other daily activities here too, such as grinding corn. Certainly many of the villagers gathered on roof tops to witness ceremonial dances which took place in the plazas below.

Immediately after World War II we visited Zuni and found a rather interesting combination of traits. A number of people virtually lived in their kitchens where some of them had modern conveniences such as stoves and sinks, radios, washing machines, and linoleum on the floor. They did have ice boxes and good wood cook stoves even in the early 1940s. The village had just received electricity shortly before our visit so many of their homes, which were previously devoid of powered equipment, were now well provided. They had abundant decoration on their kitchen walls also, particularly calendars — in fact, some had several copies of the same one hanging on their walls. In one kitchen where we visited were two signs, each saying, "I want my flowers while I live." At the other end of the spectrum was the home of an elderly lady — an interior room as traditional as could be — with a dearth of furnishings, in fact, none, only a low bench-like construction against the wall, and a ceiling which seemed higher than it was because of the room's emptiness. At one end was a free-hanging beam suspended below the ceiling supports on which the household and wearing blankets were hung. Needless to say, this lady spoke no English.

A feature of most post-Spanish areas where the Zunis have lived has been the great outdoor earthen oven or horno. With rounded top, some almost cone-shaped, this affair has a stone floor and an opening on one side. A fire is made on the floor and allowed to burn down to rich coals which are scraped out. Pans of raised bread dough, which the Zunis learned to make from white women, are shoved into the oven. A stone "door" is put in and kept secure and in place by wet rags all around. When the time comes, the "door" is removed and with long poles the hot pans with the beautifully browned loaves are taken out. The bread is excellent!

About the early homes were several age-old items. The grinding stones, metates and manos, were very important. So too were pottery vessels and a few baskets. Important also were the storerooms, chambers in which were stacked ears of corn and great pottery jars filled with foods from the fields or with wild seeds or other edibles.

Another feature of old Zuni is the kiva. Rectangular in shape, on the ground level, six of these were noted by Kroeber when he made his study of *Zuni Kin and Clan* in 1916. A few years ago we stopped at Zuni to witness the end of a summer rain dance. After the performance was over, the dancers went to a nearby building in a larger cluster of old houses, up a ladder on the outside of a doorless room and down a ladder which stuck out of the room of this chamber — the kiva.

The kiva has special features in it not encountered in the home. In particular there is an altar, a fireplace, and accommodations for the men who have gathered for the ceremony, usually a built-in bench around the edge of the room. Altars are very important parts of Zuni kivas, and are set up for specific ceremonies. When easel art first began in the Southwest about the turn of the century, several Zunis painted altars. Then as now the same major features characterized many of these centers of worship. On the wall back of the altar one artist painted the Knife-wing God, wings spread out fully and balanced symmetrically. Between his human feet is his ornate tail. Below this, on the floor, is the altar proper, of carved and painted slats of wood. An upright, wide slat on each side in the back supports a bird, crested, and with a great tail. At the top of this, between the two uprights and the back of the altar, is a wide slat painted with a snake; below is a panel on which is represented the Sun God with other figures which are cut out. At the front sides are other slats, one each to the left and right, each duplicating the snake motif but in upright position. Between these two slats are a half dozen painted objects that could represent the "dressed corn" (an ear wrapped in colored yarns with feathers sticking out the top) which commonly occurs on the floor of these altars. Extending beyond and in front of the altar is a double line, with matched round dots on each side, probably a sandpainting or the simplification of one. On either side of this painting, if so it be, is a vessel, unquestionably ceremonial; one has carved "cloud" edges plus a painted frog, common symbols of water, the other is also a cloud bowl but has a snake painted on it plus a handle over the carved edges.

In other early pictured Zuni altars there may be a basket of sacred meal in place of one of the pottery pieces, and often there are carved animal figures in front of the altars.

Bunzel reports that at the time of her work at Zuni in the 1920s (1932:518) kivas were abandoned for larger rooms. Undoubtedly the latter were more comfortable and could accommodate more villagers for certain ceremonies. She also reports other items which appeared on the altar in addition to those mentioned above. Among these are ears of corn decorated with feathers, plain ears of corn, seed-filled reeds, sacred water, prayer sticks, a variety of stone fetishes, obsidian knives, and crystal and turquoise "columns."

It was just before Kroeber's time that the Zuni began to leave the clusters of the old village. Today they have spread out to both sides of the Zuni River. Not only did they move to the north but to the south. When attending a Shalako ceremony in 1962, we went to homes where these Messengers of the Gods were staying. They were widely scattered from the northern edge of the new area to one house in the old pueblo and to several homes across the main road from the old section.

Thus it may be said that houses occupied by the Zuni today run the gamut from the original large stone-block-plastered pueblo style, to part-adobe structures, to government-built well-cut stone row houses complete with modern doors and windows, to cinder block individual houses, and last to frame structures of several rooms for individual family occupation — plus the horno adjacent to most of these homes, or the relatively new propane tanks.

Today many of these Indians have not only modern homes but modest furnishings for them. Not only are the kitchens well-equipped but also bedrooms and dining areas are comfortably set up. The village now has all the attributes of any suburban community.

A dictionary definition of economy, "the management of the resources of a community or country," especially "with a view to its productivity" would surely apply to the Zunis in the following summary.

Certainly for many centuries these Indians were almost totally dependent on the resources of their land, for there was little trade of more distant products. Shell from the Gulf of California — or rarely elsewhere — was one of the few such items. Then, of course, from 1540 on, Europeans brought new resources which definitely affected the economy of these people.

Natively the Zuni produced his own food, or hunted or gathered it. For clothing, he cultivated cotton, or used skins of animals he hunted, or gathered native plants from which he made cordage. He constructed his home from whatever materials he had at hand: stone, clay, timbers, earth. He had little in the way of household equipment, but produced ceramic pots and pans from native clays or basketry utensils made of native plants. Stone and bone provided him the basic material for knives, for hunting tools, and tools for preparing foods. Thus his native economy was concerned primarily with the barest essentials of life — food, clothing, shelter.

Economy and religion were intimately related. It was through his prayers, his religious ceremonies and dances that he brought the rains to nurture his crops, for food and fabric — to make all things grow and stay alive. Animal dances made these creatures

Pictured at left: Zuni Pueblo 1912, by Jesse L. Nusbaum. Courtesy of Museum of New Mexico. (Neg. #61739)

available to man and increased their kind.

Then came changes which affected the Zuni economy. The Spanish brought in new plants, domestic animals: sheep gave them a new food and a new material for weaving; cattle and goats, new food; donkeys and horses, a totally new way of travel. Diet was varied by the introduction of wheat, melons, tomatoes, and other products. It was much later, long after the first Europeans arrived, that the Zuni homes changed. By degrees, tables, chairs, beds, and still later, stoves, refrigerators, and other advanced equipment came to these people.

More directly related to their basic economy were other incidents. Direct contact with Anglo-Americans, particularly in the second half of the 19th century, gave these Indians the opportunity to sell pottery and some textiles. At this time also a Navajo taught a Zuni the craft of silversmithing. Although the smith made objects of this new material mainly for himself and other Indians for several decades, when he began to sell to the white man this became a major economic concern. It has been said, several times, that everyone at Zuni is involved with silver and turquoise work. Often children have been given lesser tasks connected with this craft, this in itself supporting its economic significance. Too, when top individual pieces of Zuni turquoise and silver sell for several thousand dollars, this is a sound indication of the craft's place in the economy of a tribe. Many of these Indians have made a good living in producing silver items. Some of the other crafts have had little or no economic significance. However, a word will be said about those crafts which have existed through the years in this tribe.

Pottery was of major importance to the Zuni Indians for many centuries. Long after contact with the Europeans they continued to make large plainware storage vessels — some rooms were lined with these which held food for months if not years into the future. Decorated vessels also continued to be made and used, particularly bowls and jars. However, as more tourists visited the Southwest from the 1880s on, the picture began to change. As with most tribes in contact with the white man, the villagers began to sell their wares and this made a difference in production. Too, they were exposed more and more to the white man's substitute wares, which also affected their production. But the Zunis continued to produce some vessel styles for their own use.

One piece of great interest was a ceremonial jar. This dark brown pot had a plain, bulbous body with one or two rounded openings, often on opposite sides. Sometimes an effigy of the sacred feathered serpent stuck his head out of one or both of these holes. This revered creature and the pot might also be decorated with shell and coral beads, fur, feathers, turquoise, horns, and other items. Another ceremonial piece was an open bowl with two or four spots on its side walls carved in steps, called cloud symbols. The piece was further decorated with simple black or black and red designs. In the center bottom might be a raised figure of a frog, an important symbol of rain to the Zuni. The frog plus another symbolic theme, the dragon fly, also appeared on the exteriors of jars, some dated 1880-1890. Canteens of this time were frequently ornamented with these subjects in the same way, with frogs in relief and painted dragon flies. These and the following pieces were white (which turns darker with age), with black and sometimes red decoration.

Food bowls were still made and used about the turn of the century and for several decades thereafter; their popularity seems to have dwindled in late years. Pre-1900 decoration might be wide and narrow bands of geometrics filled with fine lines over most of the interior of the bowl. A little later a solid red and black motif on the exterior was added, the latter often involving elongated triangles and bands.

Most popular of all utility forms and lingering to the present is the jar. Commonly this piece has a full, rounded body, and a short, gently curved neck, with a distinct line or several lines between these two parts. This is significant for it influenced the decorator to use different patterns on body and neck as early as 1850.

At the end of the 19th century, jars retained old decorative motifs and introduced new ones. Between 1880 and 1900 several favored themes on jars were established to continue until production of the old-style ware ceased in the 1930s-1940s. Some decorators moved in new directions, filling the horizontal space with an upper and lower row of deer with geometrics about the animals. Often there might be geometrics or a medallion in the vertical space between such rows; or elongated birds with triangular or curvilinear additions in red appear between the deer rows.

Characteristically, each deer has a life line from mouth to body interior in black or red, whether the creature is solid black or speckled. All-geometric styles continued into the early 20th century, although the animals with or without the medallion were favored.

Jar neck designs feature lines and small geometrics in red and black. Designs were often a combination of curvilinear and rectilinear themes within solids, or line-filled, or in outline. They are usually different from the themes on the body of the vessel.

One of the most appealing developments in ceramics among pueblo Indians of recent years has been the "Storyteller." This is the figure of a woman with anywhere from one to one hundred children on her — in her lap, usually, if fewer, and, as numbers increase, on her outstretched legs, clambering up her shoulders and on them, on her back, her chest, wherever a vacant spot may be. She sits there, usually with closed eyes, a round, open mouth emitting the sounds of a song or a story. Details often reflect the specific pueblo from which the potter comes, or the individual potter. Sometimes the storyteller is a man, or a clown, a Mudhead or Koshare. Sometimes the children are modeled individually, to be scattered around the storyteller.

Figurines in general would seem to antedate this specialized type; from the ancestral Zuni village of Hawikuh came such clay pieces. Again, they are to be found at Zuni proper in the late 19th century. And, of course, there is the well-known and sometimes abundant owl with one or more babies on it, a pre-1879 example with two on its back (Stevenson:1884:). Apparently these Zuni owls influenced other potters who made animal storytellers at Cochiti (Babcock:1986:39) and Acoma (ibid:Fig.28).

Owls have been very popular at Zuni for a long time, for they were commercially successful. Quite large ones were made at this pueblo in the 1880s. Through the 1940s, 1950s, and into the 1960s they were most abundant. Then they became less numerous but were still made in considerable quantities.

It is of interest that men as well as women are producing pottery at Zuni. However, this is a contemporary trend in a number of pueblos of the Southwest. Colors are often different in modern Zuni ware while forms and designs may sometimes reveal lingering tribal traits. There is, of course, much mediocre production, with many pieces in a weakened traditional style. Withal, a freshness of creativity appears frequently in some of the individual and better modern pottery of this pueblo.

To witness a line of Zuni women in "full dress" marching in the Inter-Tribal Indian Ceremonial Parade in Gallup in years gone by was to see a bit of the history of weaving in this tribe. Most obvious was the attractive dark blanket dress, this set off by white moccasins with thick, wrapped uppers. Jewelry, massive jewelry frequently, was also very much in evidence, all the more outstanding as the bright silver rested on the dark costume ground. And each lady walked in elegance as she balanced a large Zuni clay pot on her head.

A second glance caught the bright colors of the sleeve of an underblouse plus a white or colored and embroidered petticoat hanging evenly and intentionally at the bottom of the dark dress. And as the ladies passed by, one by one, each showed off another prized possession — a narrow but lovely silk paisley or flowered shawl hanging down her back. Too, one now saw individual pieces of silver, a great squash blossom necklace, large round "buttons" down the sides and in a line across the lower quarter of the dress, large dangling earrings and multiple finger rings — all heavily encrusted with small-cut turquoise. Such beauty and color and elegance can rarely be duplicated.

The dress is of long duration in this tribe, no doubt going back hundreds of years in time. Spanish contact is evidenced in the lovely petticoat, possibly in the underblouse also. Contact with and teaching from another tribe, the Navajo, shines forth in the combination of silver and turquoise. And the trading post at Zuni, or perhaps some nearby white man's town, provided the foreign scarf, which, depending upon the date of this parade, may have come from China, Portugal, or Czechoslovakia.

Let this be but the barest introduction to Zuni weaving and dress.

Although little or no weaving has been done at Zuni Pueblo for some years, if we were to go back in time far enough, to pre-Spanish and early post-Spanish years, we would encounter these villagers wearing all native, hand-woven garments. Today when the ladies dress to walk in the Ceremonial parade in August, or when they perform dances in native costume,

Pictured at left: Mission ruin and hornos, Zuni Pueblo. Courtesy of Museum of New Mexico. (Neg. #90737)

some of them have to "scrounge around" to find the proper apparel. Some families, of course, have kept the old pieces and are always prepared for such occasions.

In the prehistoric period, weaving in cotton was widespread. Some cotton fabric has been recovered at Hawikuh, which probably indicates a continued craft at this Zuni village which overlapped into the 1600s and supports Spanish reports to the effect that weaving was known in Zuni towns. Hopis started early trading of cotton garments which may well have relieved some Zuni women of this task. Occasional fibers from local plants, such as yucca and milkweed, were also employed in the weaving of small objects. From cotton were produced blankets, kilts, and some belts, and these in various weaves, judging by the general Southwestern picture.

Historical references to continued weaving at Zuni are scarce. That it continued, however, is evidenced by the many examples of weaving which have been preserved and the recollections in the minds of the people living today in this village. Contrary to the Hopi situation, much of the weaving at Zuni has been done by the women, despite the fact that men know how to weave and sometimes do so.

Zuni looms were the same as the

Hopi, vertical, and set up inside the house. Presumably, there was little or no outdoor weaving as is common among the Navajo. The Zuni loom featured a device not used by the Navajos, namely, a straight stick attached to the warp in such a manner that it could be used in keeping the fabric even throughout its length.

Among the major objects of cotton produced by the women of this tribe was a white robe embroidered in red, green, and black with a narrow band at the top and a wide one on the lower border. White kilts of cotton were embroidered in the same colors as the robes, and with cloud-rain designs.

Black wool blankets were replaced by commercial ones about 1885-90. Like many other puebloans, the Zuni also made wool blankets with stripes or bands of white, blue, brown, or black. Two types of women's shawls or dresses were made of black or dark brown wool, one embroidered on the sides, both in diagonal weave. Men's woolen shirts were also black or dark blue and done in diagonal weave. Woolen kilts had blue embroidered ends or were plain, and both types were of diagonal weave.

Although little of this weaving was economically important in terms of selling, nonetheless it was all significant in relation to supplying a woman's or a man's clothing. Today, typical American clothes are worn by the Zuni Indians.

Basketry was made before and around the turn of the century by the Zuni Indians, seldom thereafter. Undoubtedly more pieces were woven in earlier years than is apparent; as the majority of these were basically utilitarian and saw heavy service, there were probably few of them that survived to be seen by outsiders. Too, this tribe, as many others at this time, traded for baskets with other Indians. Apparently, Apache, Hopi, and Havasupai baskets were circulated rather widely in northern Arizona and New Mexico at the turn of the century. In fact, some believe that most of the baskets used by the Zuni at this time, except for certain plaited and wicker utility pieces, came from other tribes.

Jewelry has been one of the most significant economic developments among the Zuni Indians; many individuals and families have made and still make good livings following this craft. It has been said that often all members of a family followed this pursuit, including children. Inasmuch as every step in the production of a piece of jewelry was performed by the maker, all the metal work, and certainly the cutting and polishing of multitudinous stones, this was a time-consuming but rewarding task.

Zunis had little experience in metal work before the Navajos taught them silver crafting. Around the 1830s-1840s, Mexicans had given these Pueblo Indians copper and brass utensils, asking them to produce small bracelets and the like, the Indians decorating these pieces with simple filled patterns. Then in 1872, silver came to the Zuni in the form of Mexican coins first, then American coins, and, about the turn of the century, silver slugs (small squares). In the late 1920s, sheet and wire silver were made available to all Indian smiths.

Quite naturally, the first pieces of silver executed by the Zunis were the same as those made by Navajos: bridles, concha belts, canteens, the ketoh or bow guard, hoop earrings, and plain beads. It is thought that turquoise was not used in settings by the Zunis until about 1890, and then in a few, larger pieces — again, as did the Navajo. In due time, however, the Zuni acquired the proper tools with which to cut the now better stones and they began to use smaller ones. This was a natural trend for the tribe had a long history of small-stone mosaic work, in fact, this tradition went back to their ancestors in prehistoric times. The acquisition of lapidary stick, the emery wheel, and sealing wax encouraged the Zuni in these new directions in jewelry, but they were geared to the old in the design field.

More and gradually smaller stones were cut in a variety of shapes, at first round and oval, then in squares, pear shapes, and rectangles, and later in lovely needlepoint (tiny but with slender lines and pointed at each end), and petit point (tiny, slender, pointed at one end, rounded at the other). A favored style, early and late, and one involving the current shapes, was the cluster, one or several circles or ovals of stones, about a central stone. Turquoise was the favored material for cluster pieces, but coral, or even other stones might be substituted in later years. For other types of work, as well, turquoise was the main material used for some time, then shell, coral, and jet were added. New techniques were developed, with mosaic inlay growing in popularity and channel added about 1940. At the end of World War II, electricity came to the Zunis, a great boon to all lapidary workers.

Mosaic employed a variety of stones cut in different shapes to fit together — even to a tiny piece to set into a tiny hole to form a bird's eye! In channel, thin silver strips were soldered to the solid silver ground to form a pattern, anything from little squares to elaborate geometric and life form designs. Stones were cut to fit into each chamber of this "honeycomb," then smoothed off across the top. In time some jewelers rounded and polished the tops in cabochon style. Both channel and mosaic became popular and frequently were combined in a single piece.

Since the 1950s and 1960s, and particularly into the 1970s, most of the development in this craft at Zuni has been in refinement of all aspects, in betterment of design, in delicacy of craftsmanship, with many individual pieces attaining the level of fine art. Stone cutting today is so perfect that often no variation in size and shape can be noted in pieces involving more than one hundred settings, be they round, oval, square, needlepoint, or petit point. More stones were added in a single piece, again with the smith expressing great artistry through his creative hands. Gold has been acquired by these craftsmen; frequently when it is used, the artist is apt to leave more of the metal showing. In gold, smaller items, such as earrings and rings, were crafted first, later larger pieces. Traders were responsible for the first use and much of the development of gold.

Many and varied are the pieces made by the Zuni today. Several are mentioned above and some others have been added, particularly during the 1960s and 1970s. The usual rings, bracelets, earrings, and necklaces are still among the more popular pieces; so, too, is the bola tie. All of these pieces are made for sale, but also most of them are worn by Zunis and other Indians as well. A few items such as the manta pin, were made primarily for the Zunis. This pin is a large round, oval, or square silver piece, usually with a long projecting sharp point, and quite plain or decorated with much stamping or repoussé; this was a piece favored by the Zunis for the woman's dress.

Earrings have long been distinctive of the Zuni, particularly the dangling style. Often this piece has a cluster on the clip or ear portion, then several dangles, usually made up of fine chain or wire or flat pieces of silver, plain or with turquoise or other stones up and down or only at the bottom. A rather outstanding earring, often made in early years, was of wire filigree of beautiful design and exquisitely delicate. Popular indeed was the large cluster ring; this piece may also be made in the newer techniques.

Bracelets and brooches, with multiple rows of stones or in great cluster circles, were commonly made of turquoise and silver. When the new techniques came in, they became popular for these pieces, particularly in the creation of more elaborate geometric patterns of life subjects. Beautiful, colorful, and delicately created birds perch on floral branches, or munch on cherries — these were presented in a variety of materials, on both brooches and pendants. Inlay, mosaic, or channel, with no more than a metal bezel or with borders of filed or stamped silver were combined to present a wide variety of subjects. Geometrics, simple or complex, the Knifewing or Rainbow god, the sun, Shalako or any of his major attendants, or even the Apache gans or Mountain Spirit dancer, horses, owls, quail, cardinals, roadrunners, mountain sheep or bears, butterflies — these and others were subjects for decorating many pieces. The commercial popularity of this work inspired the Zuni craftsman into ever new ideas. One belt involved a different subject on the front and back of each concha, all in beautiful mosaic of a variety of materials.

Despite all the new in jewelry, Zunis continue to develop some of the older styles; also, there have been many fine women as well as men smiths. Some of these craftswomen produce the smallest, the most delicate needle or petit point, often raising stones above the usual position. Every stone is perfectly cut and polished, the silver crafting from bezels to minute outlining silver balls, is impeccable — the end result, be it necklace, bracelet, or whatever, is a work of fine art.

To return to the Zuni background, it can be noted that preceding the story of silver is the making of jewelry from stone and shell. In such materials the ancestors of these Indians, even in prehistoric times, made everything from beads to mosaics, and all have continued to this day. Much improvement has occurred through the years, with refinement in tools, better preparation of materials, and increased interest in design.

Necklaces of shell and turquoise beads ran the gamut prehistorically from ill-formed pieces to beautifully executed examples. The latter is, perhaps, best represented by a Pueblo Bonito four-strand necklace of perfectly graduated turquoise beads. Zuni Indians have reached peaks in the making of fine bead necklaces. All over the Anasazi region tiny figures of humans, animals, and birds were carved. This inheritance has also been realized in carving the so-called fetish necklaces, which are fine decorative objects and not religious pieces. These may be made from many varieties of shell, turquoise, jet, coral, and other colorful stones. An equally great variety of decorative subjects occurs on these necklaces — birds, bears, and other quadrupeds, turtles, and others.

Turquoise mosaic on wood for pendants or earrings, or more elaborate arrangements of rows of turquoise, stone, and jet on circular pieces of shell were not uncommon in prehistoric times. Zunians inherited much of this and are adept in elaborating or refining such work. New materials have been added to old favorites like coral and shells from all over the world. Of course, the base for much of this work today is silver, as well as the shell and wood of the past.

As the Zuni smith worked more on his own, with abundant and better turquoise, he began to cut down the size of individual pieces of stone and to put more of them in a single necklace or ring. Further, he might surround a single, central circular stone with a ring of the same. By the 1930s-40s, this style was made even more complicated by adding another row or two of stones, and by cutting the turquoise in squares, rectangles, or ovals. A 1930s squashblossom necklace has a pendant with a double row of turquoise, oval in form but not too regular and even. So too with the squash blossoms, each has irregular settings and tiny silver blossoms extending beyond the cluster of stones.

By the 1940s, mosaic had been developed, as is to be noted in a brooch in the form of a kachina bent in the dance. Turquoise, shell, and jet were cut rather simply and largely in rectangles, some with a slight curve to them, to represent mask, costume, and bent body. Large silver balls outline the body, evenly cut bezels delineate the arms, legs, and mask.

Many other pieces of the 1940s, and later, show great delicacy of workmanship. On another brooch, a round one, a greatly detailed bird sat on a pencil-line thin stem, with varicolored growth about, every part exquisitely executed.

The other technique, channel, developed in the late 1930s-early 40s, still later to become popular, as used alone or in combination with other styles of working. Channel, used most commonly for bracelets, might hold a single row of rectangles of shell, a double row of turquoise squares, or, later multiple rows of shell or turquoise, or with alternating pieces. These were typical of the 1940s-50s. Belonging to the early 1960s is a cluster brooch showing the trend to substitute a row of silver scallops for a row of oval stones, a pleasing balance. Another trend, and one to grow in popularity, is a matched set of a necklace, earrings, and bracelet, all three pieces often featuring beautifully crafted needlepoint. Carving, another early 1960s trend, produced a shell necklace of birds so carved as to reveal wing or head features in shades of brown while underneath all is white.

In a combination of channel and mosaic is a 1971 bird; it has flowing wings of jet with its very different head and body of white shell pointed up with turquoise, coral, and jet. A magnificent hunch-backed flute player, on a plain silver background, has a great flurry in his sash, a credit to top 1970s work. Also made were small, centered sun's heads of turquoise, shell, and jet, with great rays of shell reaching beyond, and with a red shell or black jet scalloped edge.

Bolas flourished in the 1970s with styles from a traditional oval form of alternating rows of round or petit point turquoise to a brown shell donkey about to kick. Other designs include a lovely hummingbird on a white shell background; a red coral owl sitting on a stick; a Zuni lady in traditional dress, in white, red, brownish shell, and jet, with a shell and jet pot on her head; and a munching squirrel of deep red stone with small touches of turquoise and white shell. This barely touches on the variety of bola tie designs.

During the 1970s and into the 1980s the ever-lovely cluster work continued to be produced, many pieces by master craftsmen. The greatest attribute in these is their perfect craftmanship, with stones matched absolutely in size, shape, and arrangement. Delicate touches appear, in different shapes in a single piece, as teardrop and oval, a heavy

silver wire or scallops between rows of turquoise, and very small balls of silver at edges between stones. Needless to say, stones are perfectly matched in color in these finer pieces.

A little more ornamentation occurs on some of the 1970-80 pieces. Boxes in particular may have soft, raised leaf-like edges, small silver flowers added to lids, or different decorations on the long and short sides. Absolute perfection is reached in many 1980s pieces of Zuni turquoise and silver. One necklace was so delicate, of such small needlepoint stones that it seems impossible that this work could have been done by human hands.

Thus, in little more than a century, the Zuni Indians have moved from the style of another tribe to their own distinctive specialty. Along the way they have added new techniques. They have featured turquoise and silver, although quite a few have added shell, coral, and jet to their expressions. Very few have turned to gold and other settings. Perhaps most important is their rich legacy in designing, with the adaption of old traditional ideas to totally new and different ones or of completely new concepts in silver and turquoise.

Withal, the greatest progress in silver at Zuni is in the transition from a craft to a fine art on the part of a number of these Indians.

Pictured at left: Zuni Pueblo interior, by C.F. Lummis. Courtesy of Southwest Museum, Los Angeles, California. (Neg. #33659)

In general it may be said that organization of the Zuni Tribe is in many ways comparable to other Pueblo groups but there are also differences. Typically their beliefs were those of a simple agricultural society, many of them still in evidence today, particularly in their religion. Religious, political, and social organizations are so intimately intertwined that, for the most part, they are difficult to discuss as separate entities. Many social concepts are new, some of the old persist, but in this area there are more individual than group changes.

While the political system has been adapted in some aspects to white man's ways, lingering old beliefs continue. There has been an addition to the native political organization, the Tribal Council, with the Spanish-introduced system of governor, lieutenant governor, and deputies who hold office for one year. However, ultimate political authority of the village is in the hands of the priests, for it is they who appoint the members of this council.

Zunis had the usual matrilineal organization, with marriage outside the mother's clan group. Though the clan is the basic social unit, there are no clan houses, no recognized clan heads. Clans were important in setting up family lines for ownership of sacred objects, in rain ceremonies, and in providing the priesthoods, which are hereditary through these lineages. They are not associated with kivas, and they have little or no connection with secret societies or secret fraternities. However, certain religious acts must be performed by members of certain clans.

Formerly, the home belonged to the woman, as did all the food in it. The husband and father spent much of his time at his mother's home; obviously his religious ties were through her, and he spent much, very much of his life in ceremonial participation. Too, a baby was presented to the sun, and at the age of eight a boy was initiated into a specific society which demanded duties of him from then on. Also, frequently he became involved in additional religious activities, particularly in the six kachina groups. These involved many things including prayers, songs, and dances.

Women's religious activities were not as arduous as those of the men. Basically they provided food for all ritual occasions. At the 1962 Shalako we watched them bake bread most of the afternoon of the coming of these Messengers of the Gods. That evening they were busy cutting up and cooking meat (in one home, men were helping to cut up what appeared to be at least a half a beef) and preparing other foodstuffs. Women also have the responsibility of "feeding" many ceremonial objects, a bit more time-consuming than appears at first glance. Too, women may help the men ceremonialists in many small ways.

Religion is the center of all life in this tribe. As might be expected in an agricultural society, rain is the center of many religious observances about the area. Springs are sacred, in fact, very special, as are many other spots on their land, with offerings made at some of the most important ones — this even back in prehistoric times. Father Sky and Mother Earth are venerated, as are the welcome kachinas who bring many blessings to these Indians. Clowns often accompany the kachinas, participating in the serious ceremony or making the people laugh. Often before the masked men dance in the plaza, the priesthoods go into retreat, group after group, throughout the entire summer, for four day or eight day periods, one after the other.

Ceremonies control the weather; crops grow and mature as a result of Zuni rituals. They aid the hunter in obtaining game and see to it that forgiveness is due these men from the animals hunted, which, of course, the animals are willing to give. The tribe itself continues as a result of proper religious performances. An elaborate ceremonial cycle has been set up by this group to assure all of these and other activities necessary to life.

Ceremonies revolve about the winter and summer solstices. Summer solstice ceremonies center around rain, with prayers and retreats uppermost. Winter solstice ceremonies are concerned with fertility rites and preparation for the new year by the throwing out of ashes and the kindling of new fire.

The religious organization of the Zunis is complex. First there is the Priesthood, comprised of three major priests: one of the north, one of the "above," and one of the "below." These men hold office for life; their activities include fasting and praying, mostly for rain. The "above" priest, or Pekwin determines the religious calendar by observing the rising and setting sun. Too, he proclaims the times of ceremonies. There are twelve

Priesthoods, with membership from two to six in each. These groups have charge of Rain Spirit worship.

There are six Religious Societies, each associated with a specific kiva. As a child, each Zuni male is initiated into one of these societies. All of these groups perform ceremonies.

Kolowisi, the guardian of sacred springs, is inspiration for one of the priesthoods, and this group keeps the effigy of the Sacred Serpent. There is an important Kolowisi ceremony in connection with the initiation of little boys.

Then there are Curing Societies. Membership in these, which is for life, is extended to those men and women who specifically have been cured of a disease. Not only will this group cure individuals of illnesses but also they may rid the village of pests, particularly witches.

The twelve Curing Societies are led by the Beast Gods who are the givers of medicine. Leaders in these societies are associated with the six directions, Mountain Lion of the North, Bear of the West, Badger of the South, Wolf of the East, Knifewing of the Above, and Gopher of the Below. Sickness can be removed by sucking, by the use of magical songs, by the power of the Bear. Much of curing is really related to the knowledge of curative plants. Each of the above societies is concerned with some specialty in relation to sickness. Also, each society uses an elaborate altar which remains in the room where the group meets. Altars, as noted, have carved wooden tablets, stone fetishes, and other items which are set up on floor paintings. Prayer sticks are also used in conjunction with these ceremonies.

Very important in ceremonies is the Koyemshi or clown group. These men are chosen for one year. A leader is appointed, then he chooses nine other men to serve with him. Koyemshi may participate in the serious aspects of a ceremony or they may entertain the group with their antics.

Many age-old myths and legends guide and direct the activities of the Zuni people — they lay the foundations for religious functions. Most important in their ritual observances, are the kachinas. These human performers wear masks which identify the bird, animal, or human religious personality or the sun, rain, clouds, and other elements of nature each represents, as, frequently, do the body paint and detailed costume. Masks convert the wearers into supernatural beings.

At some point in the past, kachinas came to the ancestral Zuni villages. However, legend says that always someone died when the kachinas left. Therefore these supernatural spirits decided to visit the villages no more. "Instead," they said, "we will leave our masks with these people and let their own men put them on and perform these important rituals." And so it is. Deep indeed is the belief in kachinas among the Southwestern Puebloan Indians, the Zunis no less than any others. Worship goes back for centuries as indicated on some kiva walls of prehistoric years, where masked ritualists are presented performing ceremonies.

Comment should be made here that *kachina* involves three basic concepts: first, a supernatural being; second, the masked dancer (and the Zuni *is* a kachina when he wears the mask), and third the carved, painted, and dressed doll.

Kachinas appear in the village throughout the year. They perform two general types of rituals, one held in the sacred ceremonial chamber, the kiva, and closed to the public, the second usually in the plaza and open to the public. All men participate in these rituals in one way or another, for all Zuni males are initiated into the kachina cult. At this time kachinas whip the boys twice. The children are not switched at home but this is a ritual situation and hence is acceptable.

Means of contacting the supernaturals are numerous, varied, and wondrous. Dance and song are parts of every ceremony and add power and strength in many ways. Prayers, or chants which belong to cults, are repetitive, and must be perfectly recited. Sacrifice occurs in the form of cornmeal, foods, pahos (prayer sticks), and other such items. Fetishes are the temporary or permanent residence of power.

Fetishes are very important in Zuni religion. Those fetishes kept in the hereditary homes of the matrilineal family groups of priesthoods who have charge of the Rain Spirits are the most sacred of all, for in them rests the power of the priests. At the time of the emergence, these fetishes came from the depths of the earth. Fetishes are a part of all aspects of the religion of this tribe; they enter into all religious activities. Certain

priesthoods have declined or even died out through the years and the fate of their fetishes has proven a problem. Some have been kept in homes, some have been stored in kivas, some have been buried beyond the village. Some, even, are sold to non-Indians with the greatest secrecy. (Of course, some objects are sold which are not real fetishes, although they resemble them, or at least are called such.) Fetishes are fed, be they in homes or elsewhere. As mentioned, there are fetish jars; some fetishes are kept in these and here they are fed by placing food in front of the jar. More important fetishes are larger, less important ones smaller.

In addition to the very sacred Rain fetish, there are others. Masks, both tribal and individual, are fetishes. There are carved stone hunting fetishes, these named for specific animals though not resembling them, but are general animal forms. The personal fetish, an ear of corn with feathers about it, has also been mentioned. Concretions (odd-shaped rocks) are often considered fetishes; although not as important as others, these are placed on altars. Too, they are often sold to the outsider. Then there are various altar fetishes which are animals.

Ceremonial paraphernalia includes altars, sandpaintings, masks, various figurines, large and small, pahos

Pictured at left: Wéwa, Zuni potter. Courtesy of Southwest Museum, Los Angeles, California. (Neg. #33,663)

(prayer plumes), sacred cigarettes, rattles, flutes, and drums, among other items. All of these things are sacred; some drums, even, cannot be played except for specific ceremonies. Certain of these are kept in specified places, under assigned guidance and care. Sandpaintings tend to be small, usually squares or rectangles; their content includes clouds, rain, lightning, rainbows, various animals, and certain kachinas. Smoking, or blowing smoke, is done by ceremonialists; for example, clouds are produced by smoke and the more smoke the greater the chances that these rainmakers (clouds) will work.

Again, it may be said in summary of all organization of the Zunis that there are intimate ties between the religious, political, and social. Even the Tribal Council has retained certain religious controls, stronger or weaker through the years.

A festive air reigned as we entered Zuni on a cold afternoon in December. Indian women were excitedly baking bread in their domed ovens. Everywhere these Zuni ladies were already dressed for this most important ceremonial occasion of the year, Shalako. Over native and modern dress alike were bright squares of silk, covering their shoulders and hanging down their backs — these did not interfere with women tending fires, hauling wood, cooking indoors and out, cutting meat, whatever was necessary.

My friend drove me to a spot away from the village and said, "Go stand by that fence and look straight ahead." In that direction was a stormy black cloud. Eventually six giant white figures were dramatically silhouetted against the black cloud. They stood there, distant, silent, with the slightest motion indicating that these were the ten-foot-high Shalakos the Zunis awaited. Shortly, they formed a single file and moved, more gliding than walking, slowly downhill and disappeared into a nearby field.

Back we went to the village where we witnessed several important parts of Shalako. First, the young Fire God arrived; formerly he lit a fire in front of each of the homes where the Shalako were to stay. On this occasion he "planted" prayer plumes and sacred meal in front of these homes. Fire God was a young fellow, scantily clad on this cold, cold afternoon, his body and mask painted black, with yellow, turquoise, and red dots all over. He wears nothing but a breechcloth on this frigid day.

Long Horn, or Saiyatasha, with his several assistants, also comes into Zuni. He and these others dance in various spots about the village. Saiyatasha is the Rain Priest of the Kiva of the North. His long horn is symbolic of long life for all of his people. Dressed like Long Horn but minus this distinctive feature is his deputy, Hututu, a warrior of the Kiva of the South. These and other associated ceremonialists appear, some to perform later in the evening. Also the Koyemshi, or clowns, ten of them who have been in the village for some time, will be involved with the evening performances.

As dark came on, we stood at a point above the river where we watched each of the Shalakos cross the river on an earthen footbridge. Flanked on either side by a Zuni man wrapped in a black blanket, each Shalako appeared taller than ever. Up the short hill, across the road, and into a nearby house, the first of these Messengers of the Gods was "home" for the evening. He blessed a small altar hanging from the ceiling, a larger carved and painted floor altar, then he disappeared from the room. Later he would return to dance.

There was a bench against the wall in this room, a second one in front of it. For several hours the men who sat on these benches chanted and prayed, stressing the story of creation and migration of the Zuni Indians. Several Navajo women and I, sitting on the floor at the end of the room, were entranced by this poetic presentation of several hours.

On to a second room which was in the Council of the God's house. Here were dancers and a few singers who performed for a long time. When they finished, a long line of large bowls, including several Zuni style, dishpans, and baskets, was placed down the center of the floor. All were filled with bread, most of it loaves made by the Zuni ladies, plus a package of commercial sweet rolls, then a loaf of "Rainbow" bread, and all topped with a mass of native, paper-thin piki bread. Ritualists were first served with mutton stew, bread, and coffee. A few other Indians, a half dozen or so, ate stew also out of a common bowl. A Hopi lady next to me whispered, "This is the way we used to eat all the time." Then the remaining great dishes of bread were passed to the small audience gathered to witness the dance.

A group of men, obviously the performers plus others, wrapped themselves in their black blankets, departed for a short time, and returned to the far corner of the room. Non-dancers in the group spread their blankets with a flare, like butterfly wings, to hide the performers who were donning their masks. Out came the dancers as if dropped from the skies, Saiyatasha leading the group into a dance on the now bare floor. First Long Horn did several lengths, followed by Hututu, Nadir, Zenith, and two whipper kachinas. All were masked, in proper costumes, and heavily bedecked with jewelry. On and on they danced, never tiring.

Through the now black and cold evening we walked to another ritual house. Two Shalakos were dancing here, for it was after midnight. There were two dancers here because there were only five houses to accommodate the six Shalakos. Words cannot express one's feelings on first seeing these strange creatures, so tall as to nearly touch the high ceiling, gracefully, and majestically moving back and forth to the chanting and drumming. For an unknown but enchanting length of time these two danced. Suddenly one stopped, opened his great, projecting wooden beak and clapped it four times, accompanied by a weird whoo-whoo, then rapidly six claps. Abruptly he ran to the opposite end of the dance floor, and back again.

Now we crossed the highway and went to the third Shalako house. This dancer was not performing at the moment so we left — but not before noting a small altar hanging from the ceiling which had two kachinas on the side facing the main door. The fourth Shalako house was so crowded we did not go into it, but, rather, on to the fifth and last house of these Messengers of the Gods, now about four o'clock in the morning.

When we arrived, Shalako and four Mudheads were dancing to a very vigorous chanting group. The Mudheads looked as unreal and eerie as they do in their pictures. In due time, these performers were joined by others, in particular, the Saiyatasha group. Shalako and Mudheads alternated serious dancing with sheer entertainment. The first involved measured steps, up and down the dance floor, the second was often "horseplay." For the latter, at one point, Shalako bent far over to clack-clack at a Mudhead, or he pursued the Mudhead, who was dancing backwards, until he fell in the lap of a spectator — often a Navajo Woman on the front row. The Koyemshi would pretend that the Shalako had bitten him on the arm — and on and on.

All of this went on without a break from the time we arrived until about 7:30 in the morning. It never stopped for a moment, for the chanters never let up. The chanting rhythm was powerful, it was penetrating, it urged the dancers to faster, ever faster activity. Then, at the end of a long period of serious dancing on the part of Shalako and now ten Koyemshi, the chanting stopped and the dance ended. Prayers started almost immediately. The attitude of reverence on the part of the Zunis in the audience made real the underlying seriousness of this entire ceremony.

Early in the afternoon of this second day, the "races" of the Shalako took place. One of these Messengers was stationed far in the distance on the south side of the river. Fire God came across the little dirt bridge and joined this lone Shalako. Shortly came Saiyatasha and his group, and finally came the five Shalakos, one by one, with a clacking of beaks and tinkling of bells (Plates 6,7,8). The lone Shalako came in closer, stopping on the edge of the "running" field where he was joined by the other five Messengers. Shalakos danced all the way, while the accompanying black-blanketed men walked.

Then loud singing started. Each Shalako ran from his position to a man on one side, to one on other side, then circled several men and back to his original position. After much crisscrossing of this field, all of the dancers gathered in a single line. Quickly they left one by one, surrounded by a large group of blanketed men.

The goal of the Shalakos seemed to be the small hillock where, the day before, they were first seen silhouetted against a black cloud.

Storm clouds had brewed over nearby Corn Mountain while this race was performed. Now they had withdrawn, leaving a delicate snowfall on the ever beautiful red cliffs.

— Clara Lee Tanner L.L.D.

(3)

A silver base sheet is cut to fit the shape of the kachina.

(4)

A matching bezel is hand stamped and silver soldered to the original base sheet **(3)**.

(2)

Silver base.

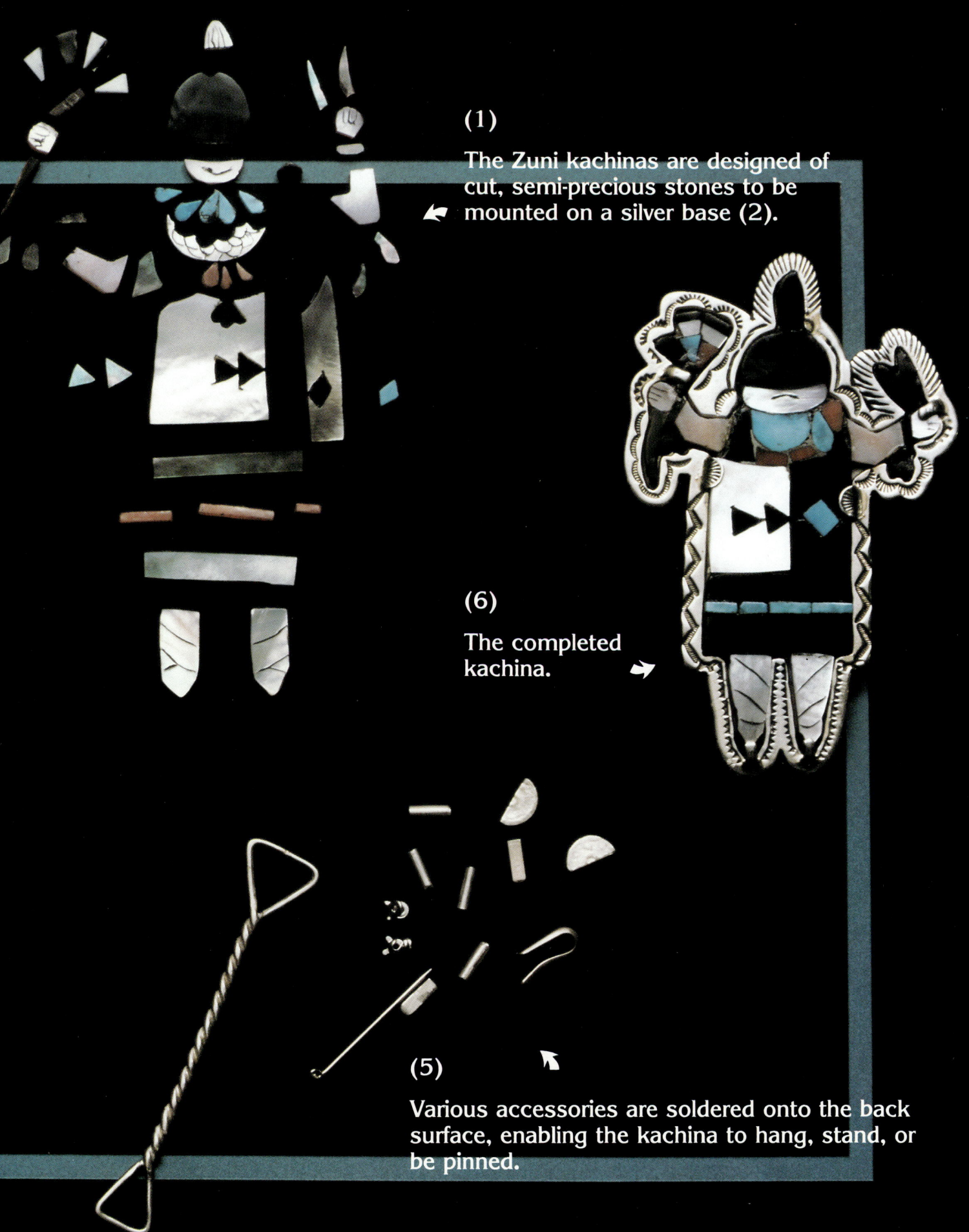

(1) The Zuni kachinas are designed of cut, semi-precious stones to be mounted on a silver base (2).

(6) The completed kachina.

(5) Various accessories are soldered onto the back surface, enabling the kachina to hang, stand, or be pinned.

WINTER SOLSTICE

Barton Wright

For the Zuni the Winter Solstice is a time for removal, for a new beginning, a clearing away of the old, and an opening for what is hoped will come. The priests mark the arrival of the New Year with a lengthy ceremony. It is one that addresses several important matters and features Pautiwa, the Chief of all kachinas, who appears but three times during the year. The first half of the twenty-day ceremony is devoted to rituals for the sun and the second half to rites for kachinas and to omens of the coming year.

The ceremony *(teshkwine)* or sacred time is announced as beginning sixteen days after the sun reaches a particular point on Corn Mountain, the large mesa to the east. Four days before this sacred time begins the members of all curing societies retreat to their ceremonial chambers to prepare for coming events.

The day preceding *teshkwine* begins when images of the Two Little War Gods are made and carried to their mesa-top positions and a bonfire made of a piece of wood furnished by each household in the village signals the beginning of a ten-day taboo against fire. During this time no fire may be made outside the home nor ashes and debris removed from inside the houses. Every person, young or old, makes prayersticks, a physical manifestation of their hopes and desires, and presents these to the spirits by placing the prayer sticks in shrines.

On the fourth day of the ceremony Pautiwa passes furtively through the town and marks each kiva and ceremonial room, sanctioning its use. Individuals who have been chosen to impersonate important kachinas or supernaturals are also sanctioned by receiving a crook from Pautiwa at this time.

In the evening before the tenth day two kachinas, Shitsukia and Kwelele from the Great Fire Society, arrive from the east bringing the New Year and participate in night-long rituals. In the morning a procession of the kachinas and other participants go east from the village to greet the sun on this final day. This parade notifies the villagers that they may now cast out the ashes and debris of the old year and prepare for the new.

The second ten-day period is one that welcomes other kachinas, the Saiyathlia, into town, and through them, cleans the last vestiges of evil and misfortune from the village. Pautiwa reappears and following a traditional circuit passes four times about the village depositing prayer objects and reading omens for the coming year. Through these actions he "makes" the New Year. Behind him come the kachinas that root out the last vestiges of sickness, those of the Great Fire Society who bring the blessings of food, and the guardian kachinas, the Salimopia, Chakwaina Okya, the spirit of their former enemy, enters town and is offered appeasement. This section for the Winter Solstice is a preview of what is hoped for the coming year.

PAUTIWA

Pautiwa, the Sun Kachina, is the leader of all other kachinas and controls their comings and goings. No kachina may go to Zuni without his permission. He organizes the ceremonial calendar and is a participant in all events even though he is seldom seen during the year. He presides over Kothluwala, the spirit village deep in the Lake of Whispering Waters, where he receives the souls of all who die. Nevertheless Pautiwa is benevolent, a kindly being who watches over the welfare of human and spirit alike and distributes his wealth with open hands to the deserving. Although he was born from the foam of a freshet and hence is a child of rain, he has exasperating, crochety grandparents and other assorted relatives. He is never in the village and when he travels about the land he often assumes the shape of a duck.

Pautiwa

SAIYATHLIA

There are two kinds of Saiyathlia. One comes during the Winter Solstice ceremony and is always represented by four kachinas. Their blackened bodies are painted, like the Feathered Water Serpent, with yellow and blue crescents and they carry bundles of yucca whips, although they are less dangerous than the one who comes at Initiation time. These Solstice Saiyathlia are guards or masters-at-arms who chastise anyone who falls asleep during the all-night rituals or they may use their whips to control individuals who become too rowdy during their entry to the Chakwaina Okya. Should anyone who suffers from headaches or has bad dreams so desire, the Saiyathlia will whip him to drive out the sickness or misfortune.

Saiyathlia

SHI-TSUKIA AND KEWELELE

Long ago in the ancient Kianankwe village of Chipia, near the mountains now known as the Sandias, there lived two kachinas. One was all white — Shi-tsukia — and the other was all black — Kwelele. It came about one time that food grew scarce and the game all disappeared. Soon the kachinas were reduced to eating their moccasins and leggings to survive. In searching for game they wandered far to the southwest and there, high in the mountains, Shi-tsukia found two maidens washing buckskins. He was so thin and famished that they took him home and fed him well, for the girls and their family had quantities of game animals penned up in stone corrals. Pretending to plant corn in the nearby fields Shi-tsukia explored farther west and found Pautiwa who was also starving. Between them they decided to free all of the game animals. Pautiwa gave Shi-tsukia a power that could help him to do this. As they were freeing the animals they were discovered whereupon Shi-tsukia blew the powder over his former benefactors turning them all into ravens who then flew away. He and Kwelele returned to Kothluwala with Pautiwa to visit before returning to their home in the east. Each year during the Winter Solstice they return to bring a new beginning to the Zuni.

CHAKWAINA OKYA

In the distant past the Zuni traveled about the land searching for the middle of the world so they might settle there permanently. During their journey they chanced one day to meet some strangers, the Kianakwe, who possessed great fields and houses but steadfastly refused to let them pass through their lands. The early Zuni, of Ashiwi, fought them. The battle was long and hard but they could not overcome the Kianakwe who were led by the giant Chakwaina Okya, or Warrior Woman, who was impervious to their arrows. At last, counseled by the Two Little War Gods, the Ashiwi succeeded in shooting her rattle wherein lay her heart, and she immediately fell dead. The Kianakwe were routed and only a boy and girl were saved and adopted into the Black Corn clan. Each Winter Solstice the Chakwaina Okya comes to Zuni to visit, going to the kiva where the Black Corn clan belongs and delivering a short talk to her people.

Pictured at left: Zuni Pueblo. Photo by Ben Wittick. Courtesy of Museum of New Mexico. (Neg. #5048)

THE OGRES

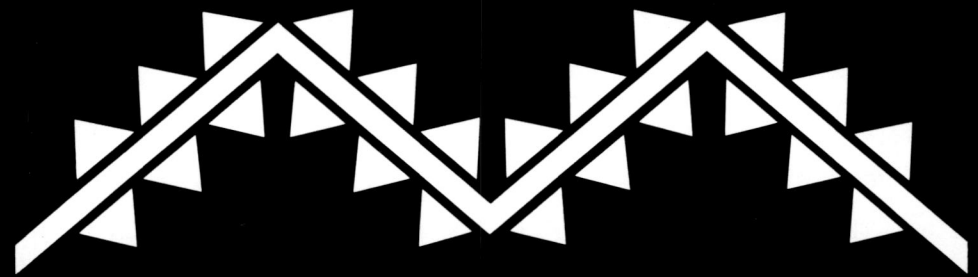

Following the Winter Solstice ceremonial there is a short period when each kiva may present either a group performance or and individual impersonation of a kachina before the round of formal Winter Dances begins. Although they no longer come, in former years this was the time when the Ogres made their appearance, usually in pairs, passing through the village and going from house to house. At each home they paused to either coerce the children into proper behavior or to frighten them into it. Besmeared with blood and with bulging eyes and vicious teeth, these creatures were horrible in appearance. They carried long sharp knives or crooks to kill or catch children and on their backs were baskets in which to haul them away. The Ogres do not live at Kothluwala like the other kachinas but instead live in caves and dens in the surrounding countryside at Zuni. At each house the shortcomings of every child was given specific and public attention and the Ogres often forced the child to demonstrate the correct behavior for the audience. During this confrontation the family or relatives supported the child by attempting to drive the monsters away through making a din beating on pans or by some other way. In the end the mother or father usually bribed the Ogres to leave by offering them other food. Unmanageable children could expect a visit from these cannibals at any time during the year.

Essentially the Ogres were a graphic representation of the very real dangers that lay in wait for the incautious child just beyond the village boundaries. In earlier days there were predators to be feared by the parents, both two-legged and four-legged, as well as the possibilities of storms or the children becoming lost in their wanderings about the countryside. When the monsters visited they emphasized the safety of home and village for it was the relatives, family and clan, who backed the children and withstood these evil creatures, forcing the monsters back to their own territory outside the village. But it was also necessary for the child to make a commitment to be certain this would occur and also to realize that he or she had duties and obligations to others and was expected by other villagers to behave in a responsible way or support might not be there the next time.

NATASHKU

The long-snouted and horned Natashku, who usually appears as a pair, is thought to be very ancient and had been brought from the Underworld by the first Rain Priest. These beings are always hungry and they look upon children as food. Waving their bows and arrows and accompanied by a gang of Koyemshi, conscripted to help them extort food, they growl and clump about the village spreading panic among the very young.

ATOSHLE

The Atoshle live in caves in the rocks north of Zuni and are cannibals who eat children. Atoshle Otshi carries a large blood-stained knife which he uses to sweep back his long matted hair from his glaring eyes. Upon reaching a house he rushes toward it four times before entering while the inhabitants try to scare him away by beating on drums and pans. Once inside he berates the children in a falsetto voice and makes them perform their duties under threat of being eaten.

SUYUKI

Suyuki haunts the peach orchards and if a woman does not watch her baby, she will steal it and put the infant in the basket on her back to take to her cave south of Zuni and eat it. She will devour a child in a single gulp. The women recognize her tracks when she is around because she goes barefoot and has long toenails. She is called to come correct only the most unmanageable children for fear her presence will kill them.

INITIATION

Every four years in Zuni, when the new moon appears three months after Winter Solstice, an initiation ceremony is held. It is a cluster of rituals designed to clean the town of any malignancy, to re-establish ties with the dead ancestors, to restate morals, obligations, and duties, to recount Zuni history, and to receive visits from the spirits who bring the promise of rain and good harvests. It is only when the town is fully prepared that it brings forth the young boys, age six to eight, who will undergo this rite of passage, their first initiation.

The event is designed to "make them valuable" for no ceremonial life is possible without it and a Zuni male is worth nothing without ritual standing. Initiation confers upon the child his first true name and introduces him to powerful supernaturals, establishing a bond that is as close as kinship. It also opens the spirit village of Kothluwala to him for should he die without initiation he could never enter that sacred place. Four years later when he is ten or twelve he will undergo a second initiation into the mysteries of the kachina cult.

The most important part of the initiation is the whipping the boys receive. Among the Zuni whipping is used only for purification, never for punishment. The rite is devised to impress the recipient with the importance and the gravity of what transpires.

Initiation actually begins with the appearance of Kiaklo and the Koyemshi eight days before the boys are involved. Kaiklo enters the town as though he had been brought by the Koyemshi from Kothluwala and visits all six kivas. At each he delivers a several hours long recitation of the creation myth with instructions from the deities to the Zuni men on their duties and reasons why the young boys should be initiated and then he leaves the village in the same manner in which he came.

Four days later the Koyemshi appear once more with the kachina Tsitsikia and work their way through the village going from house to house counting the children who will be initiated and notifying everyone of the coming event.

On the eighth day Kiaklo reappears to present a shortened version of his earlier speech and leaves in the evening, timing his departure to coincide with the arrival of Koloowisi, the Plumed Water Serpent, who appears amid great roaring made on a conch shell, and accompanied by a large crowd of kachinas.

Early in the morning of the ninth and final day Kiaklo and the swarm of kachinas pass through the town, and some over the roof tops, to purify it and bring good fortune to the young initiates. Tension mounts rapidly in the village as the kachinas rush, more and more frenzied, from kiva to kiva, moving in complex patterns as they go from one altar to another. About mid-afternoon a kachina, who has been timing the event by watching the shadows, calls out and all of the kachinas assemble with one of each kind entering the plaza where the young boys have been brought by their ceremonial godfathers. Each boy is carefully checked to see that he is wearing four blankets, then the youngsters are divided into two groups, one of which goes into a kiva to wait. The kachinas in the plaza form a line and the boys from the first group, each carried on his godfather's back, pass along the line as every kachina strikes them with a yucca whip four times. When the first group has finished they are taken to the Chief kiva to view a large sandpainting of kachinas in which many feathers have been placed and to listen to a harangue by the priests. The second group meanwhile has begun their passage through the plaza. Each initiate is asked to select a kachina in the sandpainting and as soon as all have removed their feathers from it they are returned to the plaza. It is then that the dreaded Saiyathlia appear for the final whipping, growling and clanking, leaping and charging about to prolong the interval and thus heighten the boys' fears. In succession each quivering youngster is brought forward and forced to kneel in front of his godfather between the four Saiyathlia. The first one strikes him four times with his whip and then removes a blanket from his back, a second Saiyathlia whips him four more times and removes the second blanket. They continue until all four kachinas have whipped the boy who has progressively less protection. It is a frightening and painful occasion, long remembered.

When everyone has been whipped he is again taken into the kiva where a feather is tied in his hair. In the evening when all are assembled, Koloowisi, the Plumed Serpent, thrusts his head into the kiva opening with a great roar and then vomits seeds and water on the youngsters below who hasten to collect them in bowls. This special blessing completes the ceremony of initiation after which they may return to their homes. But

each boy must avoid eating animal fat for four days and wear the feather in his hair. At the end of this period his hair is washed and a feast is held in his honor.

KIAKLO

Kiaklo, who understands all speech, was sent by his father to find the middle of the world so the Zuni might settle there. But he froze to death in the frigid north and was borne back to Kothluwala by Rainbow. Here the gods revived him and instructed him in all the history and duties of the Zuni whom he visits every four years at Initiation.

HEMOKATSIKI

Hemokatsiki is the ancient grandmother of both deities and kachinas and the only one who continues to grow old and ugly. She is their kind-hearted but poorly rewarded housekeeper and the caretaker of Koloowisi, the Plumed Water Serpent.

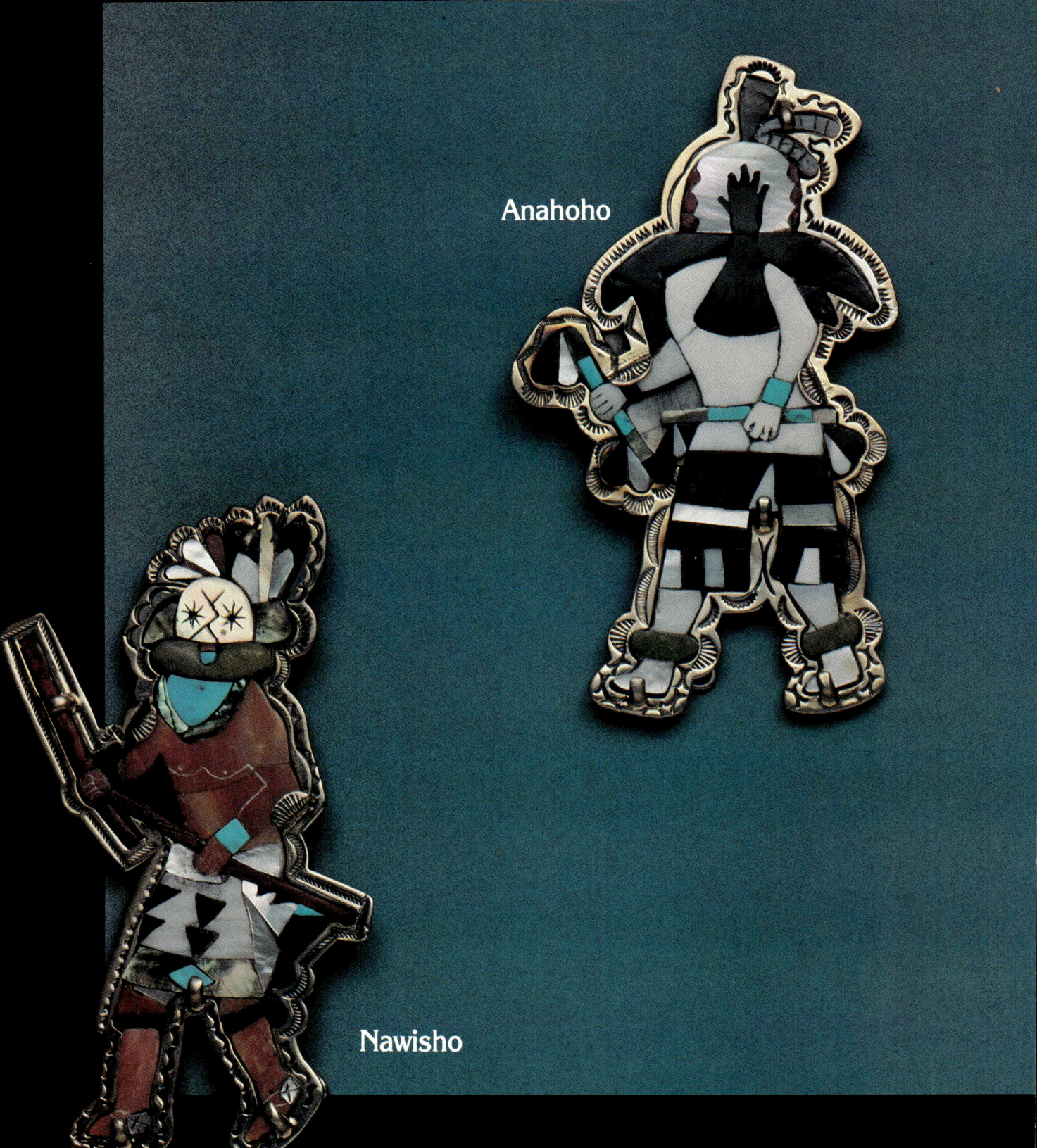

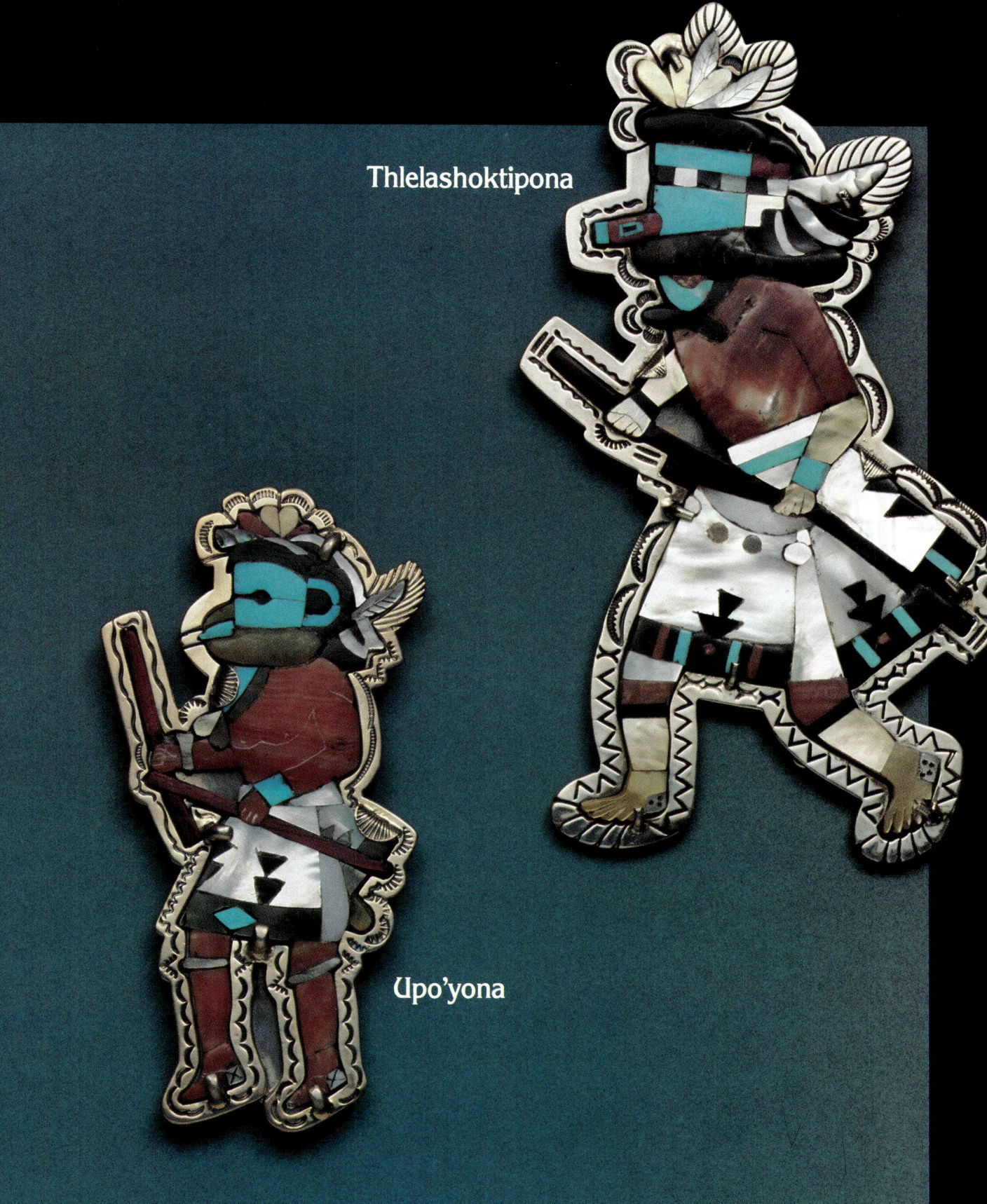
Thlelashoktipona

Upo'yona

ANAHOHO

The Anahoho are brothers of Kiaklo who were also sent out to find the middle of the world. Like him they also failed and returned as kachinas. They visit Zuni during Initiation to purify the houses in a war-related ritual of casting pottery or baskets from the roof tops.

NAWISHO

Nawisho is a pretty kachina and a fast runner. It is he who watches the church shadow during Initiation and notifies the other kachinas when it is time for the ceremony in the plaza to begin.

THLELASHOKTIPONA

Wooden Ears or Thlelashoktipona is also one of the fast running kachinas. Although his face is marked with the symbol of the Milky Way or Galaxy, he represents sweet corn and good harvests.

UPO'YONA

Upo'yona or Cottonhead is Pautiwa's young son. He comes to Zuni before Koloowisi at Initiation time and stays within the kiva. When the other kachinas call from outside he echoes their calls from inside.

SAIYATHLIA

The Saiyathlia who come for Initiation are quite different in appearance from those who come at Winter Solstice. They are believed to be more dangerous and though they come to Zuni during Initiation with the other kachinas, they remain apart. As they go about the town anyone who wishes may be struck with their yucca whips to drive out illness. This Saiyathlia will come again when the boys are initiated into the Kachina Cult.

Saiyathlia

Pictured above: Church and Bell. Photo by Ben Wittick. Courtesy of Museum of New Mexico. (Neg. #15597)

PUNITIVE KACHINAS

The boys who are initiated into the kachina cult are thoroughly indoctrinated with the idea that they must never reveal to any outsider or to the uninitiated the secrets of their society because that would destroy its meaning and value. To emphasize this and to insure their proper behavior the story of the four punitive kachinas and the boy who couldn't keep a secret is recounted.

It seems that long ago an initiated boy told someone who had not been initiated how the kachinas were impersonated by men from the village and were not supernatural spirits at all. When the kachina priests heard of this they were greatly alarmed for it threatened the value of their society and thus it was decided to call in kachinas to correct the boy. They pondered long and hard about how to punish him and who should do it and at last they chose Hainawi because of his ruthlessness as well as his friend Homatshi. Then they added two more kachinas for good measure, selecting Temtemshi and A'hute. The priests also decided that to prevent this ever happening again the only fitting punishment should be death by beheading. Hearing this the boy fled from the village and hid deep in the earth. But even though the townspeople disapproved of the harsh sentence and the Two Little War Gods, who searched for and found the boy and pulled him forth, thought he had learned his lesson, the sentence was still carried out by the four kachinas.

To this day the townspeople do not like these kachinas and shudder when they hear their calls, but there are no boys telling tales about the kachinas to the uninitiated.

HAINAWI

Hainawi is a fearsome warrior. He wears the war bandoleer that contains parts of his enemies and the warrior's feather on his head. In his right hand he carries a huge knife and yucca whips in his left. Formerly he had a white face but when he cut off the boy's head the blood spurted all over and it has remained that way. It is said that his heart is in his knife.

TEMTEMSHI

Temtemshi is a warrior and his name is taken from his cry which is so loud and shrill that it frightens those who hear it. His face and the tips of his feathers are splattered with drops of the boy's blood. He carries yucca whips in his hands but never strikes anyone.

A'HUTE

A'hute is also a warrior and he walks with a slow and ponderous step, lifting his bow and arrows as he calls out his name in a loud bellow, "A-a-a-hu-u-te!" He is the last to enter and leave the plaza when he comes to Zuni. He comes also for the Mixed Dance.

A'hute

Temtemshi

Hainawi

71

THE QUADRENNIAL DANCES

There are other important ceremonials that occur at long intervals besides Initiation. Two of these are the Kianakwe and the O'knekyanna or Ololowishkia rites. Undoubtedly they occur much more erratically, sometimes one or two decades pass between performances.

THE KIANAKWE DANCE

The Kianakwe comes for only one day every four years and then goes home. They are not thought of as kachinas because they do not live in the Sacred Lake at Kothluwala in the west, but instead come from somewhere to the south. Despite this belief that they are not kachinas the Kianakwe are very important ceremonially and their coming is awaited with great anticipation because when they arrive they bring quantities of food as presents to the priests to pay for their dance at Zuni. It is told that the Kianakwe are human people just like the Zuni and there are a number of legends telling of the first encounter of these two tribes.

In brief the early Zuni, of A'shiwi, during their long migration came upon a strange people who lived in large houses built upon the high lands who wore long white robes or dresses and spoke a different language. These Kianakwe, as the Zuni called them, had great fields of corn and other crops which the A'shiwi desired. As a result the two tribes fought for four days but neither could persevere. The Kianakwe were led by a giant woman warrior, the Chakwaina Okya, who seemed to be invulnerable to arrows and who constantly encouraged the Kianakwe warriors and rallied them if they faltered. The A'shiwi were led by the Two Little War Gods who finally appealed to their father, the Sun, for help. Their father told them that the Chakwaina Okya kept her heart in her rattle and when they succeeded in hitting it with an arrow she fell dead and the Kianakwe were routed. The survivors were adopted into the Black Corn clan of the Zuni.

KIANAKWE

The Kianakwe are led by a chief, a mosona, in this case called a Kiamosona. His costume differs from those who accompany him only in minor details. The faces of his followers are colored differently to symbolize the six directions and each carries a rattle made from a turtle shell and a bag of seeds. The dance they present differs from other Zuni dances in that it is performed in a circle rather than a line.

KOTHLAMANA

Kothlamana is a Zuni berdache, a man-woman. This kachina who was captured by the Kianakwe, dresses like a woman but is a man in strength and actions. It is believed she was a girl who refused to do women's work and enjoyed warfare. Because she was captured by the Kianakwe during their battle with the Zuni she now comes with the Kianakwe whenever they dance.

THE OKY'ENAWE DANCE

The Oky'enawe or grinding girls is also known as Ololowiskia from its principal performer. It is an eight day ceremony that occurs at long erratic intervals. When it is given it occurs on the last day of the summer dances which will coincide with the last day of the ceremony when the public performance is given. The performance is characterized by two men, dressed as kachina maidens, who grind corn in the middle of the plaza surrounded by other kachinas. The "maidens" are assisted by two Hehe'a, the blundering or Clumsy Kachina, who carry their grinding stones, corn, the blankets they kneel on, and a large bowl for each. They tend to all of the maidens needs as they grind and place the flour produced by the grinders in the large bowls. When each bowl is filled the kachina Ololowishkia moistens the flour with yucca fruit juice or peach syrup which he ejects from his enormous phallus. The resulting dough is made up into small balls by the Koyemshi who hover about and is then passed to everyone in the audience. These balls of dough are taken home and saved until they can be placed in the Zuni Fields where it is believed they will be a powerful stimulant for growth and increased fertility in the crops for the coming year. At either side of the Kokwele, the grinding women, and their helpers stands a dancer who resembles the Kokokshi and plays a flute to produce the sounds of summer. They represent Paiyatyamu, the God of Youth, Music, and Summer. To their rear dances a double line of Kokokshi, the good and beautiful kachina, or some variant of him, with their "female" companions.

Heheya

Oky'enawe

Oky'enawe

Heheya

OLOLOWISHKIA

It has been said that Ololowishkia resembles Kokopelli the Humpbacked Flute PLayer but although both are phallic Ololowishkia does not play a flute nor is he hump-backed. He has also been compared to the Water Serpent who regurgitates seeds but again this is not accurate only similar. He is probably an equinoxial kachina who brings power to produce good crops in the coming year.

HEHE'A

One of the older, more ancient, kachinas Hehe'a is one who is peculiarly inept or uncouth. He blunders about doing his duties in careless and clumsy ways so that invariably he must repeat them. His actions are usually the antithesis of what is considered to be proper behavior.

PAIYATAMU

Paiyatamu is the handsome deity of youth, music, flowers, and summer. He is fun and laughter and youth that precedes a stable maturity, a promise for the future. When he appears to play his flute the sounds that he makes are those of a warm summer with plenty of rain when the insects call and the flowers bloom, a portent of growth and good crops.

SHALAKO

THE KOYEMSHI

The Koyemshi are one of the most sacred of the Zuni supernaturals and they are incorporated in almost every ceremony that occurs. There are ten Koyemshi, nine offspring and the father. All are the result of an incestuous union between a handsome young man and his sister. In anguish at his unfortunate deed the young man wept until his eyes became swollen and he beat his head with his hands until great welts arose and all of the time he kept rolling about the ground until he changed into the lumpish character that is A'wan Tatchu, the Koyemshi Father. The nine children, who were all born in a single night, resemble their father although each has his own inappropriate characteristics and name. In action and speech these beings appear witless and idiotic as they go mindlessly about their play, yet they manage to make wise pronouncements, to announce prestigious coming events, or bring other important messages and at the same time accompany the most sacred of kachinas and amuse the audiences that watch.

Each year at Winter Solstice the Koyemshi are chosen and immediately begin a rigorous year filled with learning chants making and planting prayersticks, fasting, being in retreat for days before each event and then performing in it when it does occur. At Initiation time they bring in the demi-deity, Kiaklo, at other times they do small chores for the other kachinas, they engage in all types of buffoonery and make each effort as droll as possible.

The most prominent of the many duties of the Koyemshi is their accompaniment of the Shalakos during their year-long preparation and in the ceremony that ends the kachina season in early December. With the departure of the Shalako the Koyemshi must bring their own year to a close with a lengthy and extremely strenuous fast followed by a final performance before they too depart until next year.

Awan Pekwin

Awan Pithlashiwanni

Eshotsi

Awan Tatchu

Itsepasha

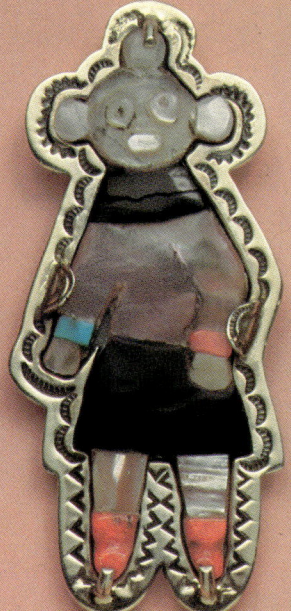

A trip to Zuñi. The Shalico dancers crossing to south side of the river

Pictured at left: Shalako Dance, Zuni Pueblo, 1897. Photo by Ben Wittick. Courtesy of Museum of New Mexico. (Neg. #16443)

The 27 participants in the Shalako Ceremony

COUNCIL OF THE GODS

All of the individuals who will take part in the great Shalako ceremony in early December are appointed during the Winter Solstice rites. Despite an intensive religious regimen that lasts for almost a full year, none of the Council members make their public appearance until the afternoon preceeding the night when the Shalako come. The first arrival is Shulawitsi, the Little Fire God, and his ceremonial father, Shulawitsi an Tatchu, who always precedes him. The two appear on the south side of the river, cross into town, and make a rapid circuit of the village, placing prayer feathers in small holes at the proper locations and recrossing the river as soon as this is completed.

As the afternoon grows late Shulawitsi and his father reappear but this time they are followed by another group. Leading this second set is Saiyatasha, the Rain Priest of the North, followed by Hututu, his lieutenant, the Rain Priest of the South. Both have helpers, a Yamuhakto who stays close by. Around the group circle the guarding Salimopia, the Warriors of the Six Directions, who keep anyone from drawing too near.

Shulawitsi rapidly repeats his earlier performance and disappears while Saiyatasha and Hututu plant their prayer-feathers and then perform a short stamping dance over the closed holes as they cry out their distinctive calls. At either side of them the Yamahakto prance with little jiggling steps and the constantly moving Salimopia patrol beyond. When they have completed this ritual they move on to the next location and repeat their performance. As they pass through the town the people come forth and cast prayer meal over them. When they have made the circuit of the village with its numerous stops, then they too disappear.

Later in the night they reappear in one of the eight special houses, after the Shalako have come. Here the two Rain Priests and Shulawitsi recite long chants and prayers that last about four hours or until midnight. This chant is a prayer for the benefit of the Zuni people. After midnight they join in the dancing which continues until dawn when Saiyatasha mounts to a rooftop for the final prayer that ends the ceremony.

Shulawitsi An Tatchu

Shulawitsi

SHULAWITSI AND SHULAWITSI AN TATCHU

Shulawitsi is known as the Speaker of the Sun or the Little Fire God. He controls fire and warmth. He is always impersonated as a young boy when he comes with the Shalako. Formerly he appeared completely nude but now he wears either a breechclout or kilt even though it is bitter cold. He carries two cedar bark torches with which he lights fires along his way as he approaches town.

Shulawitsi an Tatchu assists the Little Fire God in making with a fire drill and carries the prayer feathers during their ritual circuit of the town.

Yamuhakto

The Yamuhakto are helpers for both Saiyatasha and Hututu. Only two of them ever come and then only during Shalako. They bring firewood and building timbers and all the things that grow in the woods. This is symbolized by the wood on the crown of their heads. They also bring deer as is shown by the antlers in their hands.

Hututu

Hututu, the Rain Priest of the South, is a Bow Priest or master-at-arms for Saiyatasha, his lieutenant. It is he who attends to the more secular problems while Saiyatasha cares for the sacred. He also brings good things to the Zuni but more important he is a reinforcement of the things that Saiyatasha works for. Hututu is assisted in his duties by a Yamuhakto exactly like Saiyatasha's.

Saiyatasha

Saiyatasha, Rain Priest of the North, is one of the most respected impersonations. He controls the calendar that tells when planting should begin, when ceremonies are to be held and whether they can be postponed or not. He appears only during Shalako whose performance he orchestrates. As both a warrior and a hunter he controls enemies, the weather, even the length of an individual's life. When he comes he brings all manner of benefits to the Zuni.

Yamuhakto

Pictured above: Shalako dancers planting the Plumed Sticks, Zuni Pueblo, 1896. Photo by Ben Wittick. Courtesy of The School of American Research Collections in the Museum of New Mexico. (Neg. #16445)

The six
Shalakos

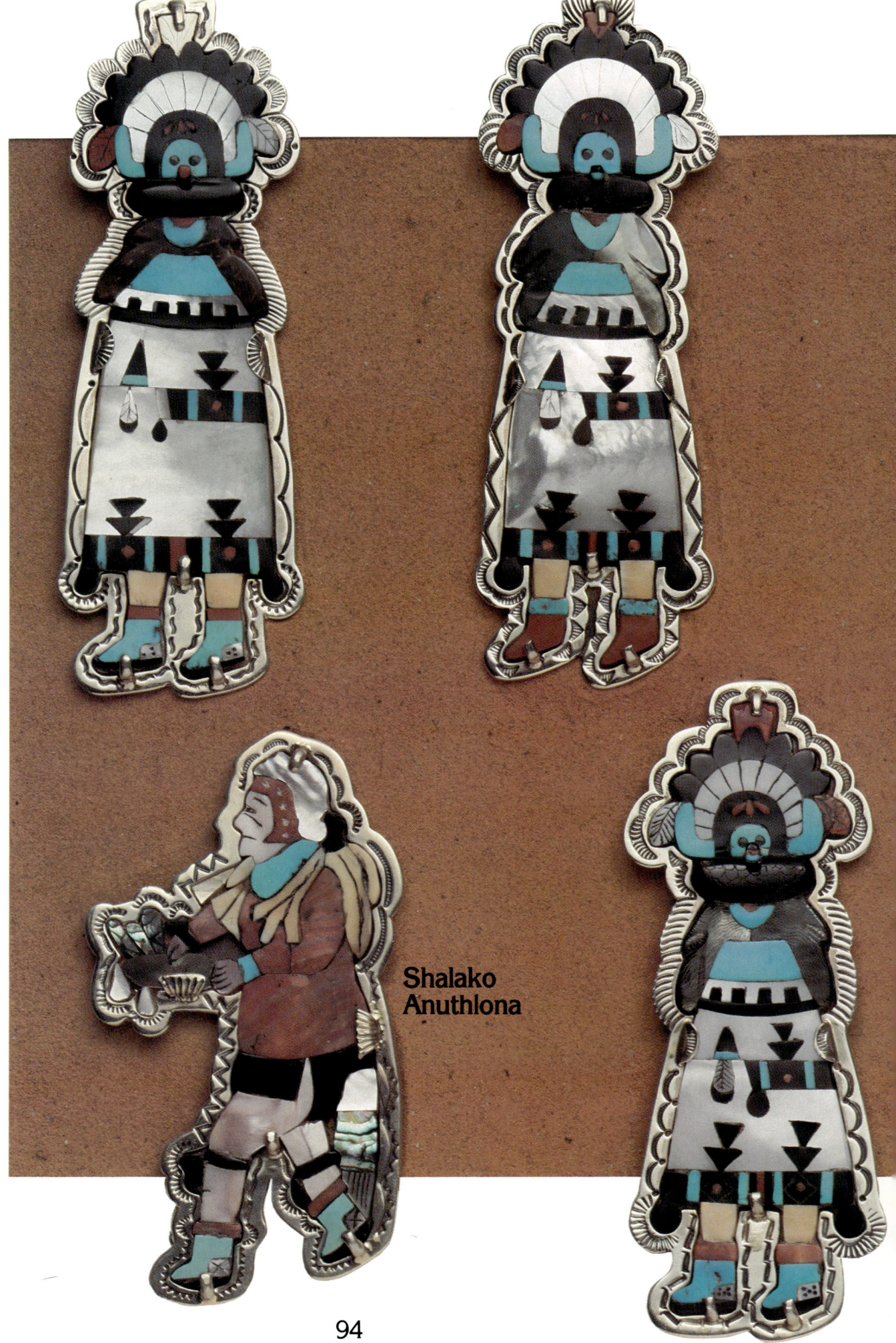

Shalako
Anuthlona

THE SHALAKO

Two men are selected from each kiva to impersonate the Shalako as it is a strenuous performance. The impersonator is required to support the 10 foot high Shalako costume and mask by gripping a pole placed up its middle. To maneuver he must peer through a tiny opening in the Shalako's middle and still be able to work the strings that will make its beak clack and clatter. In addition he must do this at night or within the confines of a house. At particular times the accompanying person, the Shalako Anuthlona, will change places with the performer so that both share equally in the task.

These men are chosen during the Winter Solstice and from then until December they spend countless hours learning chants and prayers and making long treks to various shrines to offer prayersticks. As the time of the ceremony draws nearer the pace quickens and even more pilgrimages are made. Four days before the Shalako ceremony is to begin they go into retreat. Shulawitsi's fires are the signal for the managers to take out the masks and for the actual ceremony to begin. Preparation within the village requires that there be a new house or a renovated one for each Shalako, the Council of the Gods, and the Koyemshi.

As the Council of the Gods completes their circuit of the village in the growing dusk of evening the Shalakos suddenly appear coming down the slope of Greasy Hill and approaching the village from the south. They cross the river at the footpath and pause in the dark where the effigy masks are set down on the bank and left in charge of one manager. Here they stand as though awaiting some signal from the village while the performers depart for particular houses to eat and complete their face painting. Returning they re-enter the Shalako figures and are escorted into the village by a cluster of singing men as the women line up to shower them with prayer meal as they pass. When the Shalako reaches his designated house the performer slips out and enters to bless the house, depositing seeds in an altar at one end of the room before going back out to become the Shalako and re-enter.

The first part of the night is an interval given over to a lengthy chant which recounts the creation of the Zuni and their migrations in search of the Middle of the World for their permanent home. In the process each object used by the Zuni is named and thanks offered for it. Around midnight the chanting draws to a close and the women emerge with a feast for everyone. When all have finished eating the rooms fill with people and the dancing begins. The Shalako rises from behind his screening blanket and begins to dance, swaying and bobbing, clacking his beak in time to the beat of the drum and chasing the Koyemshi who venture too close. During the early morning hours other groups of kachinas may come to dance until dawn when everything ceases as Saiyatasha completes his prayer.

After noon on the final day the Shalako and their followers reappear to retrace their steps and to perform a final ceremony on the plain south of the river. Here the Shalakos, Shulawitsi, the Council of the Gods, and the Salimopia assemble. The Shalako take turns running from six pits dug on the east of the field to six dug on the west and planting prayer plumes in each until all have completed this rite. Should one of them stumble the Salimopia would whip eveyone. The Council of the Gods then performs a similar task before the whole procession assembles and departs, returning to the place whence they came.

THE SALIMOPIA

The Salimopia are warriors and two identical ones come from each direction, hence their name, the Warriors of the Six Directions. These kachinas differ only in the colors of their heads and bodies which are symbolic of the points from which they come. They are believed to reside in the sacred village of Kothluwala until called upon to come to Zuni. The Salimopia appear only in the winter half of the year for they bring a cold wind with them when they come and this would damage the growing plants in summer. These kachinas serve as guards around the more important ceremonies or chief kachinas. Only active young, and preferably handsome, men are selected for this demanding role which keeps them constantly in motion throughout the day.

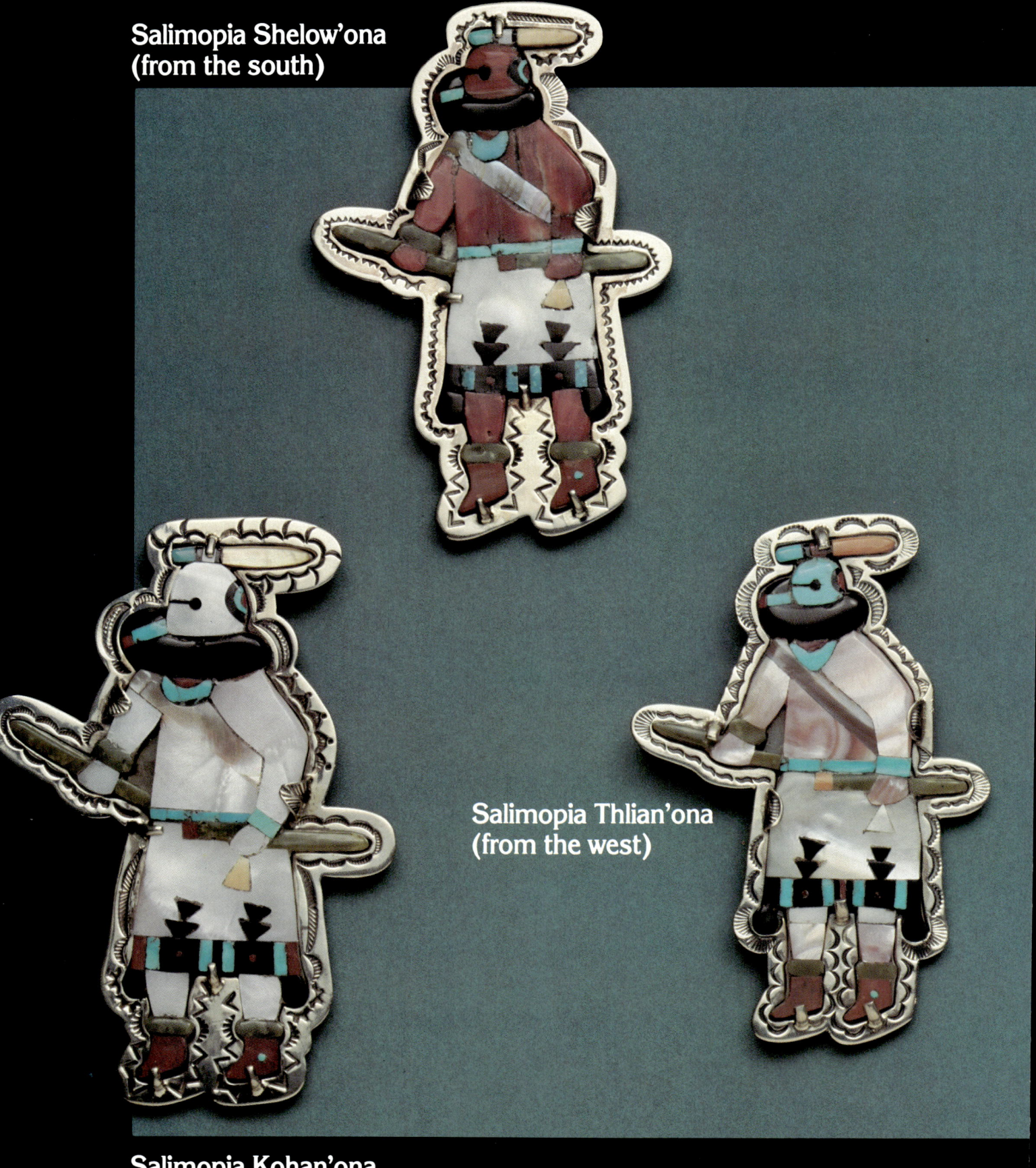

Salimopia Thluptsin'ona (from the north)

(from the zenith)

Salimopia Shikan'ona (from the nadir)

Pictured above: Shalako Dancers planting the Plumed Sticks, 1896. Photo by Ben Wittick. Courtesy of The School of American Research Collections in the Museum of New Mexico. (Neg. #16068)

WINTER/SUMMER DANCES

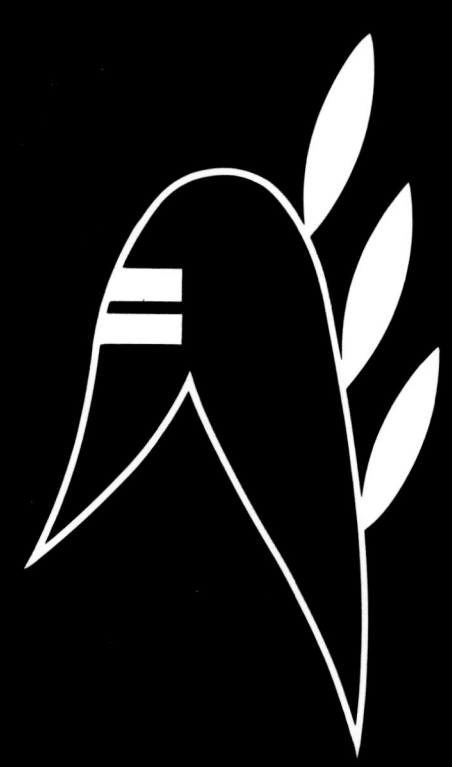

All adult males belong to the Kachina Society whose function is to present masked dances. The masked dancers represent the spirits whose powers will bring benefits to the Zuni. The membership in the society is divided among the six kivas in the village and each kiva must present dances three times during the year. One series of dances comes after the Winter Solstice and is held for fertility and increase. The other series comes after the Summer Solstice and is held to bring rain. The final series, held after the Shalako, is a "signature" of each kiva, a traditional performance before the kachinas go home.

The order of the dances to be given, but not the dates, is fixed for the winter performances and everyone is notified by the appearance of a couple of kachinas. Winter Dances formerly began about eight days after the New Year but in recent years this has been more variable. Each year a different kiva has the duty of beginning the series which rotates until all have had the duty.

The Winter Dances are held at night in the houses of the kiva chiefs and each group dances first at their own place and then visits all the other houses. Winter is also the time for trying out new and borrowed dances to gauge their effectiveness.

The Summer Dances begin with the appearance of the kachinas in the early morning dark when the men appear masked but in ordinary clothes and dance in the plaza. No one must see the kachinas at this time. Their calls notify everyone that they will reappear during the day. The kachinas come next in full costume to dance in each of the four plazas before noon and then again in the afternoon between three and four, often dancing in a single plaza.

THE KOKOKSHI DANCE

The dance of the Kokokshi is the most important of all the dancing kachinas for they attract the breath of the dead which will fall as rain or snow. As the most sacred of the kachinas each kiva must present one performance of the Kokokshi in the winter series of dances and another in the summer. However there are several versions of the Kokokshi as well as the Upikaiapona who may be substituted for them. Kokokshi variations include the Hekshina Shelowa who accompanies Ololowishkia in the grinding ceremony, The Kokokshi Tamayakwe who came from another tribe, or others. The variations are all based on small differences in the masks of the kachinas, their costumes, songs or dance steps.

As the most ancient of all kachinas it is traditional that the Kokokshi be the first given in the dances. In both instances they are accompanied by the Kokwele or Kachina Girls who dance alongside, making two parallel lines, one male and the other female, who face one way until the end of the song, then make a slow quarter turn to the right and back again. The songs these kachinas sing are quite melodic and greatly favored by the audiences. In addition they are beautiful kachinas in their white kilts and blue face masks with their long hair falling over their shoulders as the rain falls over the mesas and buttes. The feathers they wear upright on strings down their backs represent the clouds that bring the rain to Zuni.

Kokokshi

Kokwele

KOKOKSHI

The name of this being is synonymous with kachina. He is the kind and gentle kachina who brings a soft soaking rain when he dances. No matter how hard it rains they never quit dancing. It is said that these kachinas represent the spirits of the children who were lost in crossing the river when the Zuni were migrating in search of their permanent home.

KOKWELE

Kokwele is the Kachina Maiden. She comes with many kachinas but always with the Rain Dancers whether they are the Kokokshi, Upikaiapona of Hekshina Shelowa. It is they who bring in the seeds of corn and other crops for the Zuni whenever they dance.

UPO'YONA

Upo'yona is usually called Upo'yona Impiyona when he comes for Initiation but when he appears with the dancing kachinas he is just called Upo'yona. He is one of the beautiful kachinas and takes the place of Pautiwa, his father, who never dances.

KOMOKATSIKI

Komokatsiki is the Mother of the Koyemshi and she may come to Zuni when they come but usually she appears with the Kokokshi carrying in her hand the mother corn, the perfect ear.

UPIKAIAPONA

Upikaiapona or Downy-Feathers-Hanging-Down is an alternate for the Kokokshi, the good and beautiful kachinas. His costume and body color are somewhat different and details on his mask deviate slightly. No chorus accompanies him as he sings and dances but his purpose is the same, to bring rain.

DANCES AFTER SHALAKO

(TRADITIONAL DANCES)

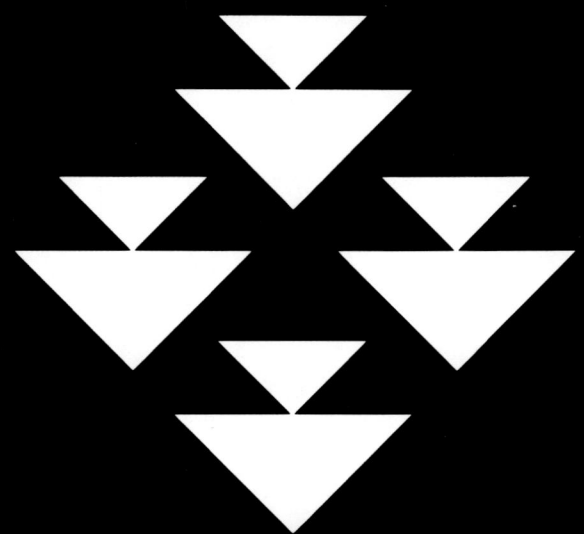

Just before the kachinas depart for their home in Kothluwala, where they will rest before returning to dance again, they give a final series of dances. Each of the six kivas in Zuni has a favored dance that it traditionally gives at this time. These dances are said to "belong" to that particular kiva. In point of fact, however, the dances may be given at anytime during the Winter/Summer series and not necessarily by the kiva to which they presumably belong. As each kiva represents a particular direction it would be expectable to see this aspect represented in the performance but neither the form nor the function of the dances seems to reflect this. Popularity of the dances changes through the years and consequently the length of the tradition is variable. For example the Kiva of the Nadir (Hekiapawa) which formerly presented the increasingly unpopular Mahedinasha began instead to give a dance known as the Old Mixed Dance of Towa Wotempthla. This in turn seems to be in the process of being supplanted by the Pasikiapa of Wide Sleeves Dance. Occasionally a kachina may be replaced or have its function relegated to another within the framework of one of these performances but this is not as common. The dances presented by the various kivas after Shalako is given in an idealized form as follows:

North Kiva (Heiwa)	Home (Towa) Chakwaina
West Kiva (Muhewa)	Hemushikwe
South Kiva (Chupawa)	Muluktaka
East Kiva (Ohewa)	Wotempthla or Mixed Dance
Zenith Kiva (Uptsana)	Laguna or Drum Chakwaina
Nadir Kiva (Hekiapawa)	Mahedinasha

HEMUSHIKWE

This tablita-crowned kachina is a part of one of the most widely distributed Pueblo dances. To the west among the Hopi he appears as the Hemis Kachina, to the east at Laguna he is the Hemish Kachina, and at Zuni he is the Hemushikwe. There are six slightly different Hemushikwe masks, unchangeable, but with the same symbolism. Their tablitas represent the clouds and the sky and their bodies the earth.

NAHALISH OKYA

The female counterpart of the Hemushikwe is either the Nahalish Okya, a Corn Girl, or the Hemushikwe Okya. She accompanies the songs sung by Hemushikwe by playing the rasper, a notched stick with a gourd resonator that is stroked with an animal scapula.

KANILONA

Accompanying the male and female Hemushikwe kachinas is usually Kanilona, the Spring Owner. His association with water is marked by the presence of frogs and lightning symbols on his mask and its dark color. He also wears feathers from summer birds on the top of his head.

MULUKTAKA

Muluktaka is one of the many forms of Corn Kachinas. He embodies all the elements required to bring growth to corn. His body is dark like the earth after a rain and he carries a staff that has eagle feathers to represent the clouds and hawk feathers to indicate rain. He wears popcorn on the ruff about his neck and it is believed that he "plants" or brings the sweet corn to the Zuni. He is also known as the Zuni Duck Kachina.

PASIKIAPA

Pasikiapa or Open Sleeves is a beautiful kachina for he comes dressed in a velveteen blouse with open sleeves of many hues and streamers of brightly colored ribbons hang from his headdress, adorn the staff he carries, and hang from the shoulders of his costume. Formerly he appeared only in the Winter Series of dances but now he comes in the dances after Shalako and seems to be replacing the Hemushikwe as the traditional dance of the West of Muhewa Kiva.

MAHEDINASHA and OWIWI

The Mahedinasha used to come in a large group early in the morning and search out anyone who had gone outside to relieve himself. The kachinas would surround the unfortunate person to taunt and then whip him. They were very nasty kachinas and no one liked them so they no longer come to Zuni. Instead the beautiful Pasikiapa now comes and dances in their stead. Late in the day when the Mahedinasha came the kachina Owiwi would appear. Owiwi is the grandfather of Mahedinasha and he is very old and bent and raggedly dressed but he is a great hunter. He makes a hunting altar in the corner of the plaza and demonstrates to the people how they should begin a hunt with the proper ceremony. It is said that he can make a young girl very rich because he owns many valuable things despite his ragged appearance.

Pasikiapa

Owiwi

Mahedinasha

113

Chakwaina

CHAKWAINA

There are two kinds of Chakwainas at Zuni, a recent import from Laguna called the Short-Haired or Drum Chakwaina and this one, the Home or Towa Chakwaina. He belongs to the Heiwa Kiva and is always danced after Shalako. He may also be substituted for the Kokokshi and appear during the summer rain dances.

It has been said that Chakwaina represents Extevan, the Moor, who accompanied Marcos De Niza on his journey of discovery to the Seven Cities of Cibola, but this is incorrect. He comes to Zuni from the east and he is a kachina who sings amusing things, often at the expense of others. His songs offer advice on every subject and because his remarks are often quite pointed he is frequently called the Unkind Kachina.

CHILILI

Chakwaina is usually accompanied by the kachina Chilili who used to be a Chakwaina also. However when he came his feet were so big, being encased in real bear feet, that he stepped on the Zuni Children and injured them. The irritated parents told him that he could no longer come as a Chakwaina but he could dance alongside of them. Because of the sound his bear claws made striking against one another, he became known as Chilili.

TOMTSINAPA

Tomtsinapa is another of the beautiful kachinas in both appearance and voice. He dances at the side of the line of Chakwaina and holds a small fir tree in his left hand. Formerly he came with the Mixed Dance to sing so that the women would sing just as sweetly when they were grinding corn as would the men who sang to the women while they worked.

Tomtsinapa

Chilili

THE WOTEMPTHLA

The two most common forms of dance groups among the Pueblos are the Line Dance, wherein every kachina is identical in costume and mask, and the Mixed Dance where each dancer represents a different kachina. Normally this latter type of dance does not feature either a line of female dancers, nor the individual kachinas that perform out of the line, the Side Dancers.

After Shalako at Zuni, two Mixed Dances are supposed to be given. Traditionally the Ohewa Kiva dances the Wotempthla or Mixed Dance. The Hekiapawa Kiva, after dropping the unpleasant Mahetinasha, substituted a dance called the Towa Wotempthla, the Old or Home Mixed Dance, which uses a drum and different songs and dance steps. Recently, however, the Pasikiapa seems to be usurping its position.

The kachinas that come in the Mixed Dance are wildly varied. Some may be pretty, others grotesque, they may be fierce or innocuous, humorous or dangerous. The only limit appears to be the choice and number of individuals involved for the inventory of possible kachinas is very large. Usually the complement of the dance will have representatives from each kachina class such as guards, warriors, plant and animal kachinas, insects, either serious or humorous characterizations of neighboring tribes, as well as all manner of natural phenomena. Occasionally there are sets of kachinas within a Mixed Dance who perform what amounts to a skit based on some mythological relationship. The basic purpose of the Mixed Dance seems to be exposure of the greatest number of kachinas possible, a visual enumeration, for it is not believed that the kachinas come to use their specific powers but rather come only as rain dancers.

AINSHEKOKO

The Zuni believe that the bear, like all animals, can put on or take off his skin as though it were clothing. Consequently the Bear may shed his skin and dress as a kachina in costume and mask, or remain as an animal when he comes to Zuni to dance, without losing any of his great powers for medicine or warfare. Since he does not fit in any of the Line Dances he can only come to the Zuni in the Wotempthla.

Ainshekoko

Ohapa

Ainshekoko

OHAPA

The Bee Kachina brings honey and insures an increase in bees when he comes. The honey was used to ease pain for teething infants and to make the priest's paint shiny. One of the Hehe's frequently comes with Ohapa and tries to get his honey with hilarious results.

MITSINAPA

Among the Hopi the Lizard Kachina is associated with sexual prowess. Although his specific function at Zuni is unknown it is probably similar in nature.

NA'LE

Legend has it that long ago the Zuni had only rabbits to hunt for meat as there were no deer in existence. Because the people were always hungry Pautiwa put the thought of deer into the priests' heads and the Hunter's Society implemented this by praying for the animal, part by part, in their ceremonies until one day the deer appeared. Since that time the Zuni have always had many deer to hunt.

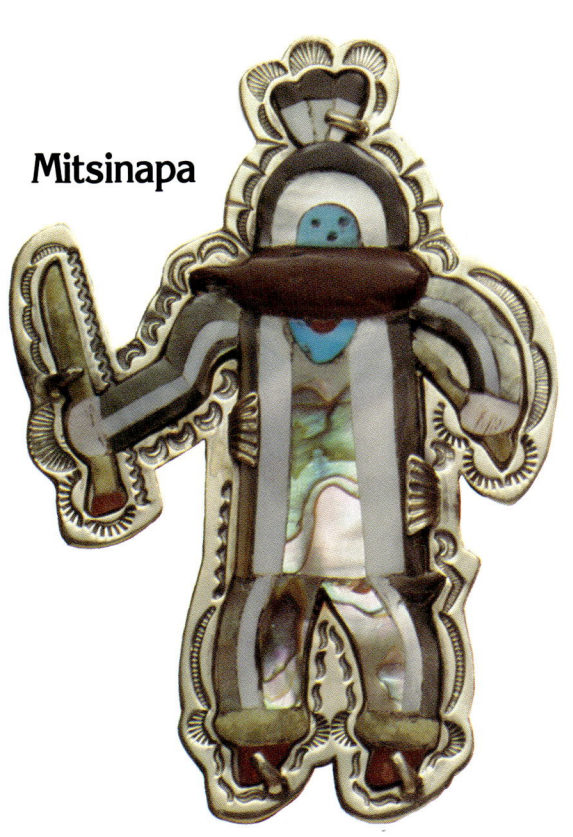
Mitsinapa

Na'le

Ishan Atsan Atshi

Hetsululu

ISHAN ATSAN ATSHI

Long ago there lived two little boys who were so poor that their home was the village dump. Because they were so dirty people called them the Grease Boys. Unable to stand their poverty they went to Pautiwa who listened to their story and then gave them fine clothes and even arranged for them to go to Zuni with the kachinas. Unfortunately Pautiwa had no shoes to give them so to ease their aching feet the boys alternate in carrying one another.

HETSULULU

Hetsululu was another poor boy who died from his misery and went to Kothluwala. Here the kachinas dressed him by painting his body with beautiful stripes of bright colors. To give purpose to his visits to the Zuni, Pautiwa gave him a game to play of flipping dobbets of mud from the end of a cone at the people who, when they were hit, saved the pellets as a prayer for fertility.

Wo'latana

This much-traveled kachina was copied from the Hopi Hilili, a bogie or scare kachina, who in turn had been taken from the Zuni Hilili. The Zuni had borrowed their version of this kachina from either Acoma or Laguna who in turn had gotten it from Cochiti.

Wahaha

This kachina was inspired by a Hopi performance called the Yahaha wherein the girls try to wrest prizes for the young men who call out, "Yahaha!" when they have a prize. At Zuni Wahaha comes with two girls and they play the same game.

Mokwala

Reputedly the kachina represents the spirit of the mountain sheep and when he dances the animals will increase. When Mokwala comes to Zuni he is nearly always accompanied by the Wolf kachina because they occur together in the wild.

Pictured above: Zuni Woman Grinding Corn. Courtesy of The Southwest Museum, Los Angeles, CA. (Neg. #33,660)

THE MOLAWAIA

The Molawaia is a dramatization of the return of the Corn Maidens by the unmasked kachina known as the Newekwe Man or Bitsitsi. The story revolves around the loss of the Corn Maidens who represent the seven kinds of corn grown by the Zuni. Through some form of disrespect to the corn such as waste, the failure to properly care for it, or to appreciate its value, the Corn Maidens decided they were not wanted and fled from Zuni. They hid so well that none were able to find them and the Zuni slowly starved. At last the Newekwe (Galaxy) Man took pity on them and came to the priests of the village saying that he would bring back the Corn Maidens if all were sincere in the desire for their return. To prove they were, the priests underwent a severe fast with many devout prayers and the planting of prayer sticks increasingly distant from the village. Convinced at last Bitsitsi hunted out the Corn Maidens and talked them into returning with Pautiwa himself accompanying them to Zuni. The Molawaia is the solemn procession of Bitsitsi, Pautiwa and the seven Corn Maidens returning to Zuni and being gratefully received by the priesthood for the benefit of all the people.

Bitsitsi

EXTRA DANCES

After the required dances have been given in either the winter or summer series other supplementary dances are presented, building slowly to a climax when every kiva will be holding a dance. There is a great variety of these to choose from and it is relatively easy to present them for the masks are not thought of as sacrosanct as are the ones which require society assistance, lengthy prayers, and numerous plantings of prayer-sticks. Instead it is in these dances that the young men can excercise their fancies with expensive or flashy costumes.

Inspiration for these dances arises from the needs of the village such as the desire for an increase in cattle which can be given spiritual assistance by performing the Cow Dance with the kachina Wakaci. A presentation of Kakali, the Eagle kachina, assists by bringing eagles to the nearby cliffs to nest. Corn, of course, is aided by numerous kachinas, probably more than any other thing. In addition, the possibility of benefit, a share as it were, of another tribe's fortune is enhanced by representations of neighboring peoples. These characterizations range from realistic to clownish caricatures, from serious to humorous. Some dances are so recent they may never have been danced before while others are old enough to have collected their own legends.

NAHALISHO

Nahalisho, the Crazy or Foolish Grandchild, received his name for killing turkeys at night and then not using them. As a Corn Kachina he appears in the Nawish or Corn Dance, variations of which appear in virtually every Pueblo. Presumably he was introduced into Zuni from Laguna sometime around 1904.

NAHALISH AWAN MOSONA

Nahalish Awan Mosona is the leader of the Nawish Dance and he carries a gambling ring in his right hand and the flute of Paiyatamu in his left. He is a side dancer in this Corn Dance.

KANATSHU

Kanatshu is a gentle dancer like Kokokshi with whom he occasionally dances. An entire set of them may appear in a Line Dance in the winter series. Interestingly when Kanatshu comes with other kachinas none will dance opposite him.

WAMUWE

Wamuwe comes in a Line Dance also and always has things to throw away or give to the audience. The drummer who accompanies him beats on a rolled up buckskin. Almost certainly he and the Hopi Kuwan Heheya are derived from the same source.

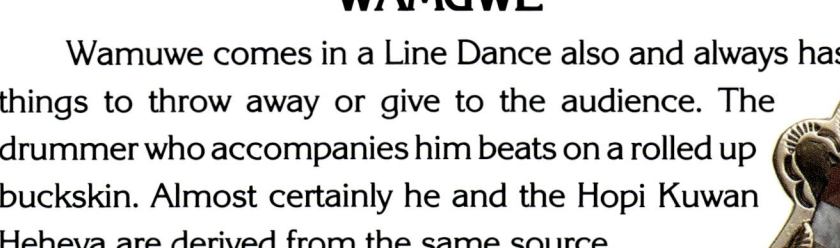

Wamuwe

Kanatshu

Nahalish Awan Mosona

Nahalisho

Ainanuwa
Ainanuwa takes care of the Buffalo during the Sioux or Lapilawe Dance.

Lapilawe
Lapilawe represents the Sioux who used to own this dance. It is danced to attract more buffalo.

A'thlanna
A'thlanna brings in the Buffalo Kachina and "kills" him during the dance.

Siwolo
Siwolo or Buffalo comes in the Lapilawe Dance to bring more buffalo.

Pictured at left: Zuni War Dance.
Courtesy of The Southwest
Museum, Los Angeles, CA.
(Neg. #33,662)

Kwamumu
Navajo Man

Kwamumu Okya
Navajo Woman

NAVAJO DANCES

Two varieties of the Navajo Dance are performed at Zuni. The Kwamumu Dance is a representation of the Navajo that the Zuni borrowed from the Hopi originators of the kachinas. The Pakoko is an original version of the Navajo Yeibichai Dancers. The male and female Pakoko are accompanied by the Yeibichai Grandfather or Navajo Talking God. It is a very hard dance to sing for as most of the songs are falsetto.

Pakoko
Navajo Yeibichai Dancer

Yeibichai
Navajo Grandfather or Talking God

Pakok' Okya
Female Navajo Yeibichai Dancer

Wakashi
The Zuni Cow Kachina who dances for an increase in cattle.

Mukikwe
A Zuni borrowing of the unmasked Hopi Powamu Kachina.

Mukikw' Okya
Female partner of the Hopi Powamu kachina but changed to a Zuni girl.

Hilili Kohana
Hilili is a fierce frightening kachina who comes to Zuni from Acoma or Laguna.

Kakali
Kakali, the Eagle Kachina purchased from the Hopi in the last century, comes to increase eagles.

Chathlashi
Chathlashi used to come with the Chakwaina. Nowadays he is too old to dance but he sings well and comes as the chorus for Hilili and other kachinas.

Wilatsukwe

Wilatsukw' Okya

APACHE DANCE

The Wilatsukwe Dance is a Zuni representation of the White Mountain Apache people who are their neighbors to the southwest. The music and steps to this dance have proven popular and it has been borrowed by all of the Hopi villages and reportedly by Laguna to the east. Both figures are dressed in characteristic Apache costumes.

LITTLE DANCERS

The Little Dancers can come anytime of the year but are seen most often in the kiva dances of winter. They are impersonated by boys and whenever they appear they are mischief makers. Hehe'a sneaks about hiding here and there until he can surprise the Koyemshi and hit them with a bag of pepper to make them sneeze. Shulawitsi Kohanna is like the real Little Fire God except he is all white. Itetsona, Double-Face, behaves like the Salimopia and carries yucca whips to use. Nahalisho, Foolish Grandchild, acts like Hehe'a but does not use pepper.

Hehe'a

Itetsona

Shulawitsi Kohanna

Nahalisho

139

SOCIETY KACHINAS

Saiyapa

Shumaikoli

SHUMAKWE SOCIETY

Shumaikoli and Saiyapa are the spirit patrons of the Zuni curing society, the Shumakwe. Formerly these two kachinas lived far to the east in the ancient mythic village of Chi'pia. Shumaikoli is a blind kachina who cures convulsions, cramps, and rheumatism. His warrior or helper, Saiyapa, lived in this world before clothing was known and formerly came to Zuni completely nude. There are six of each of these two kachinas at Zuni.

NEWEKWE SOCIETY

Kokothlanna is the Big Kachina of the Newekwe Society and lives at Ash Spring. He is a curing kachina that comes only when the society is initiating novices or when his services are needed for curing. Although Mitotasha looks like a kachina he does not stay with the others at Kothluwala but instead lives with Kokothlanna at Ash Springs in Ojo Caliente. Both Mitotasha and Kokothlanna are patron saints of the Newekwe or Galaxy Society.

Pictured above: Zuni Man in War Dress. Courtesy of The Southwest Museum, Los Angeles, CA. (Neg. #33,661)

MISCELLANEOUS KACHINAS

NATSHIMOMO

Natshimomo is a messenger who comes to mark the roads and tell the people that the kachinas will be coming in a certain number of days. Formerly he used to appear in both the Winter and Summer dances but now he comes only in the winter. He is proud of his rattle and shakes it constantly which is why they call him Grandfather Rattles All The Time.

NEPAIYATEMU

Nepaiyatemu is a clown but although he does funny things and it makes the people laugh, he is a jester for the kachinas. He can either come masked or unmasked, sometimes with a group like the Wotempthla, he may sing for one group of kachinas or come as a group himself. There is a close relationship between his role and that of Bitsitsi but in an inverted fashion.

NENEKA

Neneka is a recently imported kachina at Zuni. He is well represented in most Keresan villages to the east but his function is unknown. However at Zuni he does not have an important role as yet.

145

DEER DANCE

The Deer Dance is an unmasked dance imported from the eastern pueblos that has recently been revived at Zuni. Na'le Otshi is performed by the men and the Na'le Okya is danced by young women.

THE SCALP DANCE

The wars that existed for the Zuni were not of their own making but the result of raids by nearby or nomadic tribes. When war did occur the Zuni took scalps. But because all of the dead are rain-bringers, the enemy scalps required an elaborate 12 day ceremonial to overcome their enmity and make their potential for rain benefit the Zuni. In this complex ceremony ties between kin, clan, and societies were used to set up interwoven roles and duties and the various groups who participated. One of these was the set of two girl dancers, the Awek Suwa Hanona, the Earth Purifiers or Exorcisors, known also as Hashiya or Shakers. Planks were placed over pits dug in the plaza and covered over. On these the girls danced. The planks are considered to be doors for the people in the earth and dancing on them draws the enemy dead. The shaking of the planks makes the hearts of the dead enemy shake and tremble and makes them more amenable to Zuni desires.

Awek Suwa Hanona

Pictured above: Old Zuni Pueblo. Photo by John K. Hillers. Courtesy of Museum of New Mexico. (Neg. #22818)

SWORD SWALLOWERS

Legend tells that the Thlewekwe or Wood people split from the other Ashiwi and traveled far to the north. However, to their astonishment, when they performed their rain ceremonials it snowed and they had never before seen this. Since that time their songs and dances have produced cold rains or snows.

Continuing east they came to the ancient village of Shipapolima and there met the divinity of the Zenith, Knife-Wing, who taught them how to cure problems of the throat by swallowing wooden swords and using medicines of herbs. When they left he sent the Beast Gods of the Six Directions with them to protect their paths. Returning to the west they met the other Ashiwi at their present pueblo but before rejoining, each priest demonstrated his fetish and its powers. The other Ashiwi did not like the snow until its purpose of deep moisture was explained to them and then the Thlewekwe were accepted.

In thanks for rejoining the other Zuni they performed their ceremonial dance, which is given only in winter, and demonstrated their ability to swallow swords and cure throat problems. A boy, Thlewekwe, and two girls, Thlewekwe Okya or together called the Muyaiwe, dance in the plaza on the last day carrying the feathered swords before the other members of the Thlewekwe begin their performances.

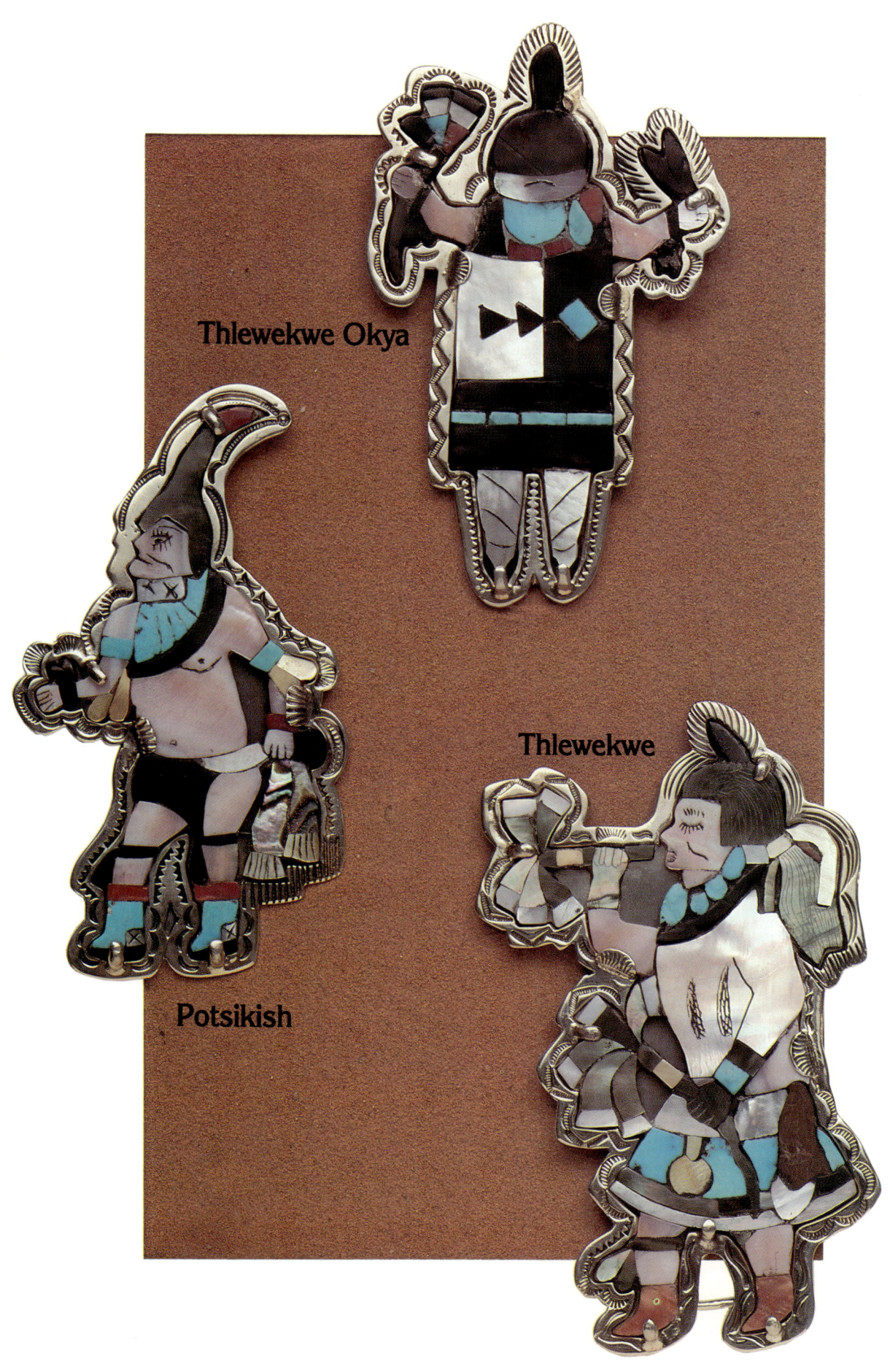

Thlewekwe Okya

Potsikish

Thlewekwe

SANTU DANCE

The patron saint of Zuni was formerly the Virgin of Guadalupe but in 1871 this image was stolen by American vandals and the figure of St. Francis of Assisi was substituted. Despite the change in gender the Zuni regard the figure as female and refer to it simply as Santu.

In early January the image is set out in the house of the santilona, the one who cares for the figure, for a period spoken of as child-bed or a time of lying-in like a pregnant woman. During this time the Zuni place small replicas of desired items made from dough about the figure in prayers for increase.

In autumn the image is again set out for a period of eight days, lying down for the first four and sitting up on the altar for the second four. During this time she is guarded by two young men who are called soldiers. Following the appearance of the santu a dance is given in the plaza in which the Sate'tshi E'lashokti appears.

Sate'tshi E'lashokti

Pictured above: Pueblo of Zuni. Photo by Ben Wittick. Courtesy of Museum of New Mexico. (Neg. #16390)

CONCLUSION

In conclusion, the satisfaction in doing this book is honoring two Native American women, Ida Poblano, a Zuni and Mary Morgan, a Navajo. These two humble and dedicated artists, although little known, have given us artistic enjoyment and understanding of their culture. My only regret is that Ida died January 15, 1987 before this book was in print.

I would like to include my thanks to my many friends whose help and suggestions have made this work more complete and interesting.
Martin Link: Editor of "Indian Trader"
Richard Rudisell: Curator of Photographic History
          Museum of New Mexico
Patrick Houlihan: Director
          Southwest Museum of Los Angeles, CA
John Davis of Arizona Lithographers
Susan Smith, Shevon Johnson and Jeff Raim from Raim, Incorporated.

—Bill Harmsen

LIST OF KACHINAS

Page #	Name	Page #	Name	Page #	Name
70	A'hute	107	Komokatsiki	151	Potsikish
128	Ainanuwa	75	Kothlamana	141	Saiyapa
117	Ainshekoko	82-83	Koyemshi	91	Saiyatasha
117	Ainshekoko	132	Kwamumu	51	Saiyathlia
64	Anahoho	132	Kwamumu Okya	66	Saiyathlia
129	A'thlanna	53	Kwelele	99	Salimopia Itapanahnan'ona
59	Atoshle Otshi	128	Lapilawe	98	Salimopia Kohan'ona
82	Awan Pekwin	113	Mahedinasha	98	Salimopia Shelow'ona
82	Awan Pithlashiwanni	142	Mitotasha	99	Salimopia Shikan'ona
82	Awan Tatchu	118	Mitsinapa	98	Salimopia Thlian'ona
148	Awek Suwa Hanona	120	Mókwala	99	Salimopia Thluptsin'ona
123	Bitsitsi	134	Mukikwe	152	Sate'tshi E'lashokti
114	Chakwaina	134	Mukikw' Okya	94-95	Shalako (6)
53	Chakwaina Okya	111	Muluktaka	94	Shalako Anuthlona
135	Chathlashi	83	Muyapona	53	Shi-tsukia
115	Chilili	139	Nahalisho	89	Shulawitsi
82	Eshotsi	127	Nahalisho	89	Shulawitsi An Tatchu
71	Hainawi	127	Nahalish Awan Mosona	139	Shulawitsi Kohanna
76-77	Hehea	110	Nahalish Okya	141	Shumaikoli
79 & 138	Hehe'a	83	Nalashi	129	Siwolo
63	Hemokatsiki	118	Na'le	59	Suyuki
110	Hemushikiwe	147	Na'le Okya	71	Temtemshi
119	Hetsululu	146	Na'le Otshi	65	Thlelashoktipona
135	Hilili Kohana	59	Natashku	151	Thlewekwe
90	Hututu	145	Natshimomo	151	Thlewekwe Okya
119	Ishan Atsan Atshi	64	Nawisho	115	Tomtsinapa
139	Itetsona	145	Neneka	83	Tsathlashi
82	Itsepasha	145	Nepaiyatemu	107	Upikaiapona
135	Kakali	117	Ohapa	65 & 107	Upo'yona
83	Kalutsi	76-77	Oky'enawe (Girls)	120	Wahaha
127	Kanatshu	79	Ololowishkia	134	Wakashi
111	Kanilona	113	Owiwi	126	Wamuwe
63	Kiaklo	79	Paiyatamu	136	Wilatsukwe
75	Kianakwe	133	Pakoko	136	Wilatsukw' Okya
75	Kianakwe Mosona	133	Pakok'Okya	120	Wo'latana
105	Kokokshi	113	Pasikiapa	90	Yamuhakto
142	Kokothlanna	50	Pautiwa	91	Yamuhakto
105 & 107	Kokwele	83	Posuki	133	Yeibichai